SMART
MARATHON TRAINING

SMART
MARATHON TRAINING

RUN YOUR BEST
WITHOUT RUNNING YOURSELF
RAGGED

JEFF HOROWITZ

Boulder, Colorado

▼velopress®

3002 Sterling Circle, Suite 100
Boulder, Colorado 80301-2338 USA
(303) 440-0601 · Fax (303) 444-6788 · E-mail velopress@competitorgroup.com

Distributed in the United States and Canada by Ingram Publisher Services

Library of Congress Cataloging-in-Publication Data
Horowitz, Jeffrey.
Smart marathon training: run your best without running yourself ragged / Jeff Horowitz.
     p. cm.
Includes bibliographical references and index.
ISBN 978-1-934030-74-5 (pbk.: alk. paper)
1. Marathon running—Training. I. Title.
GV1065.17.T73.H67 2011
796.42'52—dc23

                              2011034210

For information on purchasing VeloPress books, please call (800) 811-4210 ext. 2138 or visit www.velopress.com.

This paper meets the requirements of ANSI/NISO
Z39.48-1992 (Permanence of Paper).

Cover design by Heidi Carcella
Cover photo by Andy Batt
Interior design and composition by Anita Koury and Chris Davis
All exercise and running drill photographs by Brad Kaminski; gym shots taken at RallySport Health and Fitness Club, Boulder, CO
Other photographs by: p.55 (top), SIDI America, Inc.; p.55 (bottom), LOOK Cycle USA; p.62, Precor Inc.®; p.63, Saris Cycling Group, Inc.; p.154, j/fit; p.155 (top), The Stick; p.155 (bottom), Fitterfirst; p.201, Jeff Horowitz
Illustrations, tables, and training plans by Charlie Layton

Text set in Proforma

12   13   /   10   9   8   7   6   5   4   3   2

Contents

Acknowledgments

MY THANKS BEGIN WITH MY WIFE and partner, Stephanie, who has supported all of my mad schemes and crazy dreams. I don't know why you put up with me, but it's been a fun ride, yes? Thanks also to Alex, our 6-year-old son, for his boundless energy and love. Look, Daddy made a book with pictures! And thanks to my sisters, Marlene and Dori, and their families for, well, everything.

My heartfelt thanks also go out to the great crew at VeloPress: Casey Blaine for her guidance, hard work, great humor, and friendship; Kara Mannix for all her attention to details; Dave Trendler for spreading the word; and Ted Costantino for welcoming me into the VeloPress family of authors.

I also owe a big thanks to all of my colleagues at Washington Sports Event Management: Chuck, Molly, Chris, Michelle, Kristen, Dawn, and everyone who works with us. You've helped me turn a passion into a career. From the Nations Triathlon to the DC Tri to our nonprofit labor of love, ACHIEVE Kids Tri, there's never a dull moment!

Thanks, too, to the people I sweat with, the far-flung members of AOAT: Adrian, Marty, James, Tom, Kevin, Ty, Skip, Willie, Max, Stue, and everyone else who has wandered in and out of our orbit. If you look closely, you'll see yourselves all through the pages of this book.

Thanks to Frank Nasta for his constant encouragement, patience, and mostly good advice over the years.

Thanks most of all to my parents, Louis and Muriel, for making the hard job of raising a family seem so easy. Neither of you was a runner, but I know you'd have loved to have seen this book. I miss you both.

Introduction

"YOUR BONES WILL TURN TO DUST."

I'd been a long-distance runner for about six or seven years when a friend of mine—a *nonrunner*—said that to me.

I'd run my first marathon back in 1987. I didn't feel the need to run it again the following year, but by the next fall I was back at marathoning. Then I ran two marathons in the same year, which conventional wisdom said was the body's 12-month limit. But I felt fine after that second marathon, and I felt very motivated to get back out there again, so I decided to run a third one that same year. I finished the race feeling strong; my legs didn't fall off, and nothing was broken, strained, or swollen. That's when I began to question some of that conventional wisdom.

Over the next few years, I ran four, then five, and, ultimately, eight marathons in a single year, in addition to half-marathons, 10-milers, 10Ks, and 5Ks. Plus training, of course. I had my share of blisters, but nothing worse than that.

It was around that time that my friend made his prediction about what the future had in store for me. Given my racing volume, it wasn't an entirely crazy thing to say, I guess.

Except that I knew that he was wrong. I knew my body better than anyone else: its tendencies, its aches, the things it hated, and the things it loved. And my body loved long-distance road racing. As long as I was motivated, had no injuries, and felt strong, I saw no reason to deprive my body of that pleasure. Eventually, I ran as many as 14 marathons in a single year, sometimes on consecutive Sundays, week after week after week. I got faster, too, qualifying for the Boston Marathon and usually placing in the top 10 percent of any race I entered.

But I wasn't winning anything. I knew that to hit my peak as a marathoner, I probably had to pare down my racing. I would have to target a single marathon each season for one supreme effort.

I considered doing just that, but I realized that running a single, gloriously fast race wasn't the most important thing to me. I loved the marathon *experience*: the crowds, the journey, the finish lines. Whenever I heard about a race I hadn't run, I was captivated; it sounded like a dessert that I absolutely had to try. I wanted to experience as many of them as I could, and so I chose to enjoy the experience instead of going for the impressive personal record (PR). That was the kind of runner I decided I would be.

Eventually, my running would take me all over the world, to race starting lines in all 50 states and in places as far-flung as China, Antarctica, Africa, Thailand, and the Himalayas. I saw many wonderful places, met some amazing people, and experienced life in a way some people only dream of. I felt like the luckiest man in the world. I still do.

I didn't want to keep this experience all for myself, so I became a certified running coach and personal trainer. Over the following decade, I introduced hundreds of people to the thrill of completing their first half-marathon or marathon or, if they were already experienced, to running their new personal best.

DURABILITY: ART OR SCIENCE?

There are two kinds of long-distance runners: the kind who admit to having been injured and the kind who don't. I didn't bother to deny anything; I ended up with my fair share of injuries. In fact, much of my knowledge of physiology is rooted in having to learn about a part of my body after hurting it. But all of these injuries were transitory. Everything healed sooner or later, especially after I'd analyzed why I'd gotten hurt in the first place and made the necessary adjustments to keep it from happening again.

And now, with over a quarter century of road racing behind me, including 150 marathons and ultramarathons, my bones are as solid and strong as ever. These days, no one predicts that my body will fall apart. I've been doing this for too long for anyone to dispute that it can safely be done.

Instead of predicting doom, people wanted to know, how did I manage to stay healthy and whole while doing all this running?

I wondered that myself.

The numbers seem daunting: Every marathon involves something on the order of 40,000 steps to complete, and every step puts up to four times my body weight of 155 pounds on each foot. The totals are frightening: My 150 marathons alone—not counting all of my training runs and other races—have required me to take about *6 million steps*, inflicting a total of *3.72 trillion pounds* of pressure on my feet, knees, hips, and back.

How could my body possibly take all of that pounding?

People insisted that I was superhuman. I liked to think so, but my wife would have disagreed, and she'd have been right. But I will grant myself this: I'm fairly unusual. You won't meet too many people who have run as many long-distance races as I have, for as many years as I have. I've managed to do it all without having any great gifts as a runner. Even if I'd focused my training on getting as fast as possible, I never would have become an elite racer; I just never showed that spark of quickness that could have been fanned into great speed. And my consistency as a runner—my strongest characteristic as an athlete—isn't record-setting, either. I'm not even among the top 10 most prolific marathoners alive today, and the world record for the most lifetime marathons run is more than 10 times what I've achieved.

But I have raced a lot, more than most of the serious runners out there and far more than any doctor would say should be humanly possible. Every orthopedist I've ever spoken to has warned me about how bad my running routine is for me and about how my body must surely be on the verge of collapse.

Once, for example, I went to see an orthopedist shortly after running several marathons and a 50-mile ultramarathon within a few weeks. I was experiencing hip pain, and even though common sense told me that I was probably just sore and tired, it was a new ache, and I thought it wouldn't be a bad idea to get the ache checked out.

After the appointment, I wasn't so sure of that.

The orthopedist examined me and pronounced my hip shot. "Your marathoning days are over," he said. I explained that the problem felt more muscular than skeletal, but he insisted. Who was I to tell a doctor that he was wrong?

Here I was again: *Your bones will turn to dust.* After listening to this orthopedist long enough, I began to wonder how I'd actually managed to run a marathon at all because he made it seem so utterly impossible. But I had to keep in mind that the only runners most orthopedists meet are the ones who come to their clinics with battered bodies; the healthy ones never stop by to say hi. If an orthopedist sees only hurt runners, maybe he comes to believe that all running hurts.

I also considered how happy the doctors all seemed when they reviewed my overall health profile. They were quick to point out how all my numbers were in the normal range or better, sometimes much better. How did they think this came about? Magic and wishful thinking? If running were so bad for me, how had it managed to make me so healthy?

I decided to prove the doctor—and all doctors like him—wrong. My hip didn't feel like it was about to collapse, and I wasn't about to give up running without a fight. Yes, there are times when injuries and other limitations cannot be overcome by sheer determination. But as a rule of thumb, I'd rather assume that I *can* do something and be proved wrong than to not even try. If I accepted conventional wisdom about my limitations, I'd never have found out what I was truly capable of. So after resting up and then getting back into my fitness routine, I returned to marathoning and ran several more ultras as well.

TRAINING SMART, RUNNING HEALTHY

My marathoning days were hardly over. How then could I explain my durability? The relevant literature didn't seem to have answers. I had no problem finding studies about the physiological changes that occur during a single training cycle: how the body adapts to additional mileage by increasing its blood volume, its energy-producing mitochondria, and its ability to make better use of abundant fat stores for fuel. But I couldn't find anything that would explain why my body was holding up so well over so many years.

Then I had a realization. Most runners who got injured didn't hurt themselves in a *race*; they hurt themselves in *training*. Ask any injured runner about the origin of his or her problem, and the reply usually goes something like this: "Well, it was about a month before my race when I began to feel a twinge in my (hamstring, calf, knee, hip, foot), and it only got worse by race day."

How often I *raced* wasn't the real issue, then. The secret to my ability to stay healthy had to do with what was happening *between* my races.

I began to think more about what I was doing. Or, as the case turned out, *not* doing. I wasn't beating myself up while training. I got myself in marathon shape, and then I did only what I needed to do to stay there and to be as fit as possible *and no more than that.* This might sound like a sensible, even obvious approach, but for most runners it's neither reasonable nor obvious. We're a stubborn breed by nature; we wouldn't be able to run for hours if we weren't.

Long-distance running is based at least partly on an ability to endure discomfort. Because of that, it tends to attract people who, like me, are stubborn. Before too long, we begin to define ourselves by how much pain we can take and how grueling our workouts are. "Pain is nothing," the popular mantra goes. "It's just weakness leaving the body."

Perhaps. Or maybe it's really the sign of a muscle or ligament about to tear.

The gravitational pull of doing bigger and longer workouts is hard to resist, however. There is a feeling among runners that if a little bit is good, a lot more must be a lot better. Once, years ago, I read about elite runners who typically run more than 100 miles a week. I thought, *they must know what they're doing*, so when I decided to use my next marathon to qualify for the Boston Marathon and a possible personal record, I tried running high mileage, too. I ran twice a day, as I'd read all the elite runners do, and I got my mileage up to 80 and then 90 miles per week.

I felt proud of what I was achieving—I was training like an elite runner, wasn't I? But I knew that this wasn't the best of my running. I was dragging my body through two workouts a day, and I was slow, tired, and unmotivated. Still, I kept up with my plan, sure that I was doing the right thing. I just had to get through this, I thought, and then it will all feel better.

What I didn't consider was that elite runners get hurt all the time. I was probably lucky that in trying to copy them, I didn't hurt myself, too.

When race day came, I felt confident that I would do well. And I did. I didn't set a new PR, but I did qualify for Boston. I was pleased, but I had to admit that I hadn't really done any better than when I had trained on half that total mileage.

Meanwhile, I was struggling with a problem I was having as a coach for a charity running team. Most of my runners hit their targets, whether it was finishing their first marathon or achieving a personal best. But invariably some of my athletes got injured. Not very many, statistically speaking—just one or two a season—but that was enough to concern me.

For all the benefits of running—or of any kind of training, for that matter—there's always a risk of getting hurt. That just comes with pushing your body beyond its comfort zone. I knew that, and so did all of my clients and team members.

But still, it was hard for me to see any of my runners get injured, especially when they were relying on me to keep them healthy and strong. I knew that I'd written and implemented a training program based on reasonable, widely accepted training principles, and I had not exposed my runners to any unreasonable risk, but I still couldn't help but feel responsible. I kept asking myself, *could I have done anything differently?*

I thought about the running magazines I subscribed to. The cover of almost every one of them offered advice on how to deal with hurt knees, Achilles tendons, iliotibial (IT) bands, and hip flexors. I realized that most runners were either in the process of recovering from an injury or on their way to getting sidelined by an injury.

There had to be a better way.

There was. I had to flip the notion that "more is better" on its head and instead commit myself and my runners to setting a mileage limit and making the most that we could out of the miles we ran. We would aim to achieve everything we wanted from our running by doing less. Why would we do more than that?

I devised a plan that includes three runs a week, totaling no more than 35 miles, consisting of speed and hill work, a tempo run, and a long endurance run; core strengthening, strength training, running drills, and balance work two to three times per week; and aggressive crosstraining, recommended as cycling, at least twice per week.

I presented this plan to my clients and found that they not only were able to avoid injury, but they also were able to run stronger. I then shared this plan at talks I gave at race expos and wrote about elements of it in articles. Now I want to share it with you.

This plan is intended to bring common sense back to running. You may not want to race as many marathons as I have—or run a marathon at all—but you should be able to run the races you choose pain-free.

WILLS AND WON'TS

Before we begin talking about what this book will do for you, let's start by talking about what it won't do:

- It *won't* guarantee that anyone can stay injury-free. No one can guarantee that.
- It *won't* guarantee you a PR. There are too many variables to make that promise.
- It *won't* get you to a race finish line without your doing any hard work. There's no way to fake a marathon. Indeed, that's actually something that many of us love about it.

But here's what this book *will* do for you:

- It *will* help you run as pain-free as possible, given your body's mechanics, genetic inheritance, and health issues.
- It *will* help you get to your next starting line feeling good and strong, which is 90 percent of the battle.
- It *will* help you minimize the risk of injury and give you a plan for dealing with injuries that do arise, turning them into speed bumps in your training and racing plan instead of insurmountable roadblocks.
- It *will* help you get the most from the running that you do and put you in a position to go for a PR if the conditions are right.
- Most importantly, it *will*, I hope, bring more joy to your running.

There's nothing fun about running below your potential or struggling with injuries. When things go bad with running, frustration sets in, and the happiness we discovered when we first began running gets obscured or lost.

Getting our health and speed back is the best way I know to rediscover that happiness.

This book is about becoming a smart runner, about *consciously* and *purposefully* making reasoned choices in how you train and race.

As with any good training plan, it is a tool for you to use. Like any training plan, however, it involves commitment to a philosophy. I don't ask for blind obedience, but if you do want results, you're going to have to commit to fully trying this plan and judging the results after a season is over. And you're going to have to work hard.

That shouldn't be too much to ask. I've never met a distance runner who was afraid of a little hard work.

HOW TO BEGIN

The first step is to evaluate yourself as a runner. The programs presented here can apply to anyone training for a half-marathon or marathon, whether it's the 1st or the 40th, but the common denominator is that the reader is already a dedicated runner. This book is not for absolute beginners. Before you attempt a higher-intensity training program, you need to build up a solid base of endurance, muscle strength, bone density, and strong ligaments and tendons. That comes from consistent running over a period of months to years. So if you're brand new to running, focus initially on building up your mileage slowly and steadily before using the training plans in the Smart Marathon Training program.

Do you need to have already run a distance race in order to use this book effectively? No. Plenty of elite runners aim to race competitively in their debut half-marathon or marathon. I myself ran a marathon as my very first race, mostly because I felt that I needed a big scary goal to really focus my training. So even though it would be ideal for you to have run some long-distance races already, don't worry if you don't have that on your athletic resume yet. As long as you've developed the appropriate training base through months or years of running, you're on solid ground. Read on.

You may have already run one or more distance races and want very much to improve while staying healthy. You may have had a few injuries. Or maybe the training program you were using didn't seem able to help you get to the next level. For all these reasons, this program is for you.

As to how to approach this book and your training, there are several steps I recommend.

Target your race. Decide as early as possible what specific marathons or half-marathons you'll aim to run during the coming year. Many runners train hard but without a clear goal in mind. Often, they sign up for races on a whim or out of a desire to run with their friends or training buddies. There's nothing particularly wrong with this approach, but if you are aiming to run a really good race, or even PR, that method is not much better than just throwing a pair of dice. If you want to have your best marathon or half-marathon, take out your calendar, circle some dates, and then train *specifically for those races*. This will make racing less of a game of chance and more a matter of calculating how to achieve your peak for race day.

Hitting your goals is what this book is about. It aims to help all long-distance runners, specifically targeting those athletes tackling the marathon and half-marathon. You already know how I feel about the marathon, but I have a great deal of sympathy for the half. It's a fantastic distance, short enough to allow for a hard sustained effort but long enough to require careful pacing and energy management. It requires runners to balance power against endurance in a way that no other distance does.

Whatever race distance you decide on, circle a date on a calendar, set a goal time, and register for the race. This will be explored in greater depth in Chapter 6.

Read this book. Your serious training begins with reading this book. Spend time reading and absorbing the information and training plans that are in here. Do not skip a section; each is an integral part of the plan.

Design your training plan. Use the sample training plans included here to set up your own training schedule. It might be necessary for you to tweak the program to fit your needs. That's ok. In Chapter 6 we'll talk about how to make changes that accord with the program rather than undermine it.

Plan for recovery. After running your race, you're not done as a runner. Take good care of the body that has just served you so well by following a good post-race recovery plan. For too many runners, this means simply waiting for any soreness to fade and then starting up again. As with your race preparation, you can get better results from your recovery if you act proactively and purposefully. This book will show you how.

Part of your post-race plan should include taking the time to appreciate what you've accomplished. If you keep pushing yourself to improve without stopping to reflect on how far you've come, you can end up forever dissatisfied and risk burnout. You've worked hard and raced smartly, and you've earned the right to be happy about what you've done.

But then it's time to get back to work. Too much patting yourself on the back can lead to complacency, and part of the reason you're reading this book, after all, is probably because you want to see how much better you can be as a runner. So when you're done giving yourself your propers, start thinking about your next goal. Perhaps you want to further improve your times and see what your true potential in the full or half-marathon might be. Or maybe you're ready to take on a new kind of race. As the owner of a strong, healthy body, you've got options.

So let's get to work.

The Plan

LET'S GET THE BASIC *WHAT* AND *WHY* OF THIS PLAN right on the table so that you can keep them in mind as you read the *how* that follows. Here's what you can expect to be doing on a weekly basis under this plan:

- Three runs a week, totaling no more than 35 miles, consisting of speed work or hill repeats, a tempo run, and a long endurance run
- Core strengthening, strength training, running drills, and balance work done two to three times per week
- Aggressive crosstraining, recommended as cycling, at least twice per week

Why this plan? Because too many of us get hurt too frequently doing the sport we love. That's not acceptable, and it's not the way things have to be. You may be reading this book because you believe that a change in your running program is a good idea, which also means you've already got an open mind about trying a new program. Or you may have come to this program because you've had too many injuries or a chronic injury that won't go away.

You're not alone. Most runners sustain an injury at some point that keeps them sidelined. For many of them, the cause is not hard to find: too many miles spent running, with not enough recovery. The high-mileage example comes right from the top: Elite middle- and long-distance runners routinely top 100 miles run per week and often reach over 120 and 140 miles.

Just where did this mania for piling on mileage come from? Often it's hard to identify the origin of a widespread trend, but in this case it's not too difficult: coaching legend Arthur Lydiard.

A native New Zealander, Lydiard revolutionized the running world in the 1960s by introducing long, slow runs into his training program. He emphasized the benefits of building a huge endurance base. This provided great improvements in running economy, which is a measurement of how much oxygen the body requires to run at a given speed. High oxygen consumption is a sign of oncoming fatigue, so good running economy means that less oxygen is used to run fast. High-volume running brings improvements in this measurement.

Lydiard's program required all of his runners—including sprinters and middle-distance runners—to log a minimum of 100 miles per week. His program included more than just this base-building phase, but the high-mileage requirement was always its defining component. From this philosophy was born the general consensus that to be a good runner, an athlete had to nearly always be running. Six days, seven days a week, often twice a day.

It would seem hard to contest Lydiard's program because of the results it produced: three of his protégés medaled at the 1960 Rome Olympics, and one, Peter Snell, hit double gold in the 1964 Tokyo Olympics.

Nevertheless, a few coaches, like famed coach Jack Daniels, began to question Lydiard's program. They began to put more emphasis on the intensity of the training effort instead of just the mileage. "Adding more and more mileage to your weekly training does not produce equal percentages of improvement in competitive fitness," Daniels argued. Long, slow running generally produced long, slow races, they argued. And although high mileage worked for some runners, Daniels argued that each body was different and that each runner had to discover and appreciate his or her limits (Daniels n.d., 2005).

So is it true or isn't it that only high-mileage running can produce successful long-distance runners? Consider the Africans. Road-racing fans have watched the rise of African long-distance runners since the great Ethiopian runner Abebe Bikila won the gold medal in the marathon in the 1960 and

1964 Olympics. Since then, Kenyan and Ethiopian runners seem to have been conducting a private duel in most of the world's top races, from New York to Boston to the Olympics.

This has led many American runners to wonder what it is about the African approach to running that has garnered these runners such success. Part of the reason, no doubt, is that many of these runners live and train at high altitude, which forces their bodies to learn how to work harder with less oxygen. Plus, the African culture and daily lifestyle revolve much more around running than does American culture. But the fact that these runners follow high-volume training plans has led many observers to conclude that high running mileage is necessary to achieve any success.

Still, I suspect that there's a part of the puzzle that's been missing. Even though successful African marathoners might run high mileage, it doesn't follow that every African runner can do high mileage. For every successful African runner we see winning or placing in the major races, there might very well be scores of runners back in Africa whose bodies are not able to tolerate the rigors of high-mileage training. But we rarely see in the popular press data about the injury rate of the rest of the African runners, so the myth grows that only high mileage can produce successful long-distance runners.

If you conclude from all this, however, that I believe that high mileage is always bad, you'd be wrong. For the many elite runners whose bodies can handle it, high-mileage training has yielded astounding fitness and success. Other coaches, Daniels included, agree that high mileage can be beneficial where appropriate.

The problem is that for many of us, high mileage has brought stress fractures, patella tendinitis, iliotibial band syndrome, Achilles tendinitis, and a host of other maladies, not to mention the frustration of not being able to do the thing we love at the level we'd like to do it. Or, depending on the injury, at all.

This dilemma isn't limited to middle-of-the-pack runners; many elite runners who prosper with high-mileage training also fall prey to injury. Former world record holder Khalid Khannouchi swung like a pendulum between record-setting performances and disabling injuries, and the fastest American female marathoner to date, Deena Kastor, was sidelined after suffering a stress fracture in the Beijing Olympics. Even for many elite runners, high-mileage training is often not a sustainable lifestyle.

Here's the problem in a nutshell: To run better, you have to run more. Runners need to run. That's called specificity of training. You can't be a better runner by playing racquetball, no matter what other health benefits might come from that activity. And alongside that fact sits this conundrum: To improve in any activity, you need to practice that activity, but when you do nothing but that activity hour after hour, you raise the risk of developing a repetitive stress syndrome and other overuse injuries.

But you don't have to settle for one extreme or the other. You can improve your running economy without battering your body.

This book presents an alternative to high-mileage training. It focuses on quality runs over quantity of miles, supplemented by other activities that not only produce better overall fitness but also develop the kind of strength that wards off running injuries. By running less frequently and at a lower volume while running more purposefully—and developing balanced strength—you can run better and be stronger and healthier.

Although much of the running and coaching community still sticks by the older method of training, which calls for running six to seven days a week, building up to 60, 70, or more miles per week, there's a growing body of evidence supporting the view that less is often more. Research has linked the relationship between mileage and injury onset and has established that as the miles pile up, so, too, does the rate of injury. For example, a 2007 *British Journal of Sports Medicine* review of running injury studies found strong evidence that running more than 40 miles per week increases men's risk of lower extremity injuries, especially to the knees, from as low as 19 percent to as high as 79 percent (van Gent et al. 2007).

Clearly, then, there's a point at which most runners top out on the benefits of running, after which more miles bring more harm than good. Research shows that this point hovers somewhere around 35 miles per week (Eyestone 2007).

All this seems pretty straightforward, so the question, then, is, why do so many runners continue to log more than 35 miles per week?

There's no single answer to this question, but here's what I suspect: We're stubborn people. We wouldn't be distance runners and marathoners if we stopped every time we got tired or sore. I don't know if running distance makes people stubborn, or if stubborn people are drawn to distance running, but in the end these just seem to go together. If we believe that running more than 35 miles per week is what it takes to become better, many of us are willing to live with the pain and injuries that come with that. At least up to a point.

We love to run. As a coach, I used to get frustrated when my athletes would resist doing things that I knew would make them better runners, like strength training, core training, and crosstraining. But then I had a stunningly simple epiphany: The reason for this resistance was that they just loved running. They didn't get into running so that they could do these other things, so the more time they had to spend doing nonrunning stuff, they believed, the less time they would have to run.

That makes sense, but the bigger picture is that for many runners, a failure to do all the necessary nonrunning activities will lead to an end to running as well. We think that the rules don't apply to us. When you become a marathoner, you instantly become part of a very select group. Even if you earned your medal in a race with 20,000 to 30,000 other people, you still belong to a group comprising less than 1 percent of the U.S. population. You are probably an oddity to your friends and family, and you take pride in that. You begin to believe that you're special. And you are. But you can get hurt like anyone else.

I'm guilty of this myself. I would hear about people who had the full menu of classic injuries, from plantar fasciitis to patella tendinitis to sore backs and strained hamstrings, and I would think, "That's sad, but that's not something that could ever happen to me."

My running friends apparently think the same way as I do. Many of them seem unable to make the connection between their training routine and the injuries they develop. They seem to think of their injuries not as a direct result of something they did—or failed to do—but as freak accidents, like slipping on a banana peel. I guess that would be called denial.

To progress as a runner and to reduce the risk of injury, you need to get over these roadblocks. You need to become smarter than you are brave, more reasonable than you are stubborn. You need to recognize that, although you love to run, it's possible to have too much of a good thing. In economics this is called the Law of Diminishing Returns, according to which desirable things usually lose their value in direct proportion to their increased availability. As my college economics professor liked to put it, his first burger was delicious, the third one not so much, and the fifth one was pretty terrible. This is true in running as much as in the marketplace.

You also have to recognize that in order to keep running, you have to do all the necessary nonrunning training that will make that possible. Although I hope that all runners will come to find this training program as enjoyable as I have, you must recognize that, like it or not, these are just activities that you have to do if you want to run to your potential.

No amount of wishful thinking will inoculate you against reality. The body is capable of wondrous things, but when we act like we have no limits, we act foolishly and dangerously. This book is an effort to restore reasonableness to your running program when you are faced with the limits of your body.

GUIDING PRINCIPLES

Rather than jump right into charts detailing daily mileage and workouts, I want to first lay the foundation for what follows. Understanding the principles that undergird the program will help guide you in making any necessary adjustments.

1. **Get the most for the least.** When I first presented the principles of this program at a talk I gave at a large marathon expo, I couldn't help but notice the reaction of a woman sitting in the front row. When I announced that it's possible to fully prepare for a marathon by running no more than 35 miles per week, she slowly shook her head from side to side, a frown on her face.

    I wasn't the least bit upset by this reaction. To the contrary, I was thrilled. I expected my presentation to spark some disagreement, and I was looking forward to a chance to defend my theories. The last thing I wanted was a quiet, compliant group. Without any disagreements, how could I be sure that they were even listening?

So when I saw that woman in the front, I smiled. It was clear that she considered 35 miles per week to be too small a base on which to run a marathon. Perhaps she thought that I was promising people something for nothing.

Her mistake was in assuming that running was the only component of the program, that if I cut back on running, I would shrink the time spent training. In fact, all I was doing was making running one component of a training program—the most important component, to be sure, but just one of the parts.

I don't believe in shortcuts. One appeal of long-distance racing is that there is no way of faking fitness. A runner may be lucky to get good weather or may have chosen a flat, fast course, but he or she still has to run for one or more hours. Any runner who attempts a long-distance race without properly preparing courts disaster.

Worse still, this failure can't be hidden. On race day, it becomes clear who did their homework and who didn't. Hitting the wall is no myth; it's a real physiological event that occurs when the body runs through its glycogen stores. Glycogen is the body's preferred source of fuel—it burns cleanly and is readily available as blood sugar. The body stores about a two-hour supply of glycogen in the liver, more than enough for most of its needs.

Problems arise, however, when we ask our body to work harder than we've trained it to do, especially over long periods of time. When we eat through our available glycogen stores, we experience a sudden drop in energy. It's as if our power cords were just cut or we suddenly were running through cement. The loss of energy can come on suddenly, like a car running out of gas.

That's hitting the wall.

A runner who hits the wall suddenly slows from a run to a shuffle or even a walk. It's a very public declaration that the runner didn't prepare for the kind of race she or he was trying to run.

Hitting the wall isn't inevitable, however. Long runs done in training trigger an adaptation response in the body, forcing it to rely increasingly on fat for fuel instead of just glycogen.

Fat is not the body's preferred source of fuel because processing it requires some additional steps, but there is ample fat in even the leanest body to fuel many hours of high-intensity work. Whereas glycogen requires water in order to be stored, fat does not, so the body stores it very efficiently. Fat also is twice as calorie dense as glycogen, logging 9 calories per gram, as opposed to 4 calories per gram of glycogen, so a little can go a long way. So even though most people might think of fat and calories as something to be restricted in dieting, fat is in fact an important—and for runners, a crucial—measurement of fuel. That is, if the body can be taught to use it.

All of this was on my mind when I told the expo audience that I recommended running no more than 35 miles a week. I felt confident making that statement because I knew that it is possible to trigger the body's fat-burning potential without running the body into the ground. The key is to include runs that achieve that end.

Similarly, it's possible to do runs that target speed. Most experienced runners know this and incorporate these runs into their program. Where my approach differs from other programs, however, is that I have runners do only enough running to trigger those responses, but not one step more.

2. **Make the workout count.** Along with long runs and speed work, many veteran runners log a lot of additional running. Although the benefits of long runs and speed work are clear—and I'll talk about the benefits of those runs in the next chapter—what do these other runs achieve?

I can point to a few benefits. One is to maintain overall fitness. Our bodies work on the principle of conservation, maintaining only the amount of fitness needed to accomplish the tasks we ask of it. When we ask for more, the body improves, but when we ask for less, the body relinquishes some of those hard-earned gains. By the body's logic, there's no need to carry around extra muscle or to maintain an expanded blood supply unless we might actually need them sometime soon. If our weekly running consisted only of one day each of long running and speed work, our bodies would ramp up fitness levels but would not effectively maintain them at the highest possible levels.

A second benefit, as discussed earlier, is that consistent running improves running economy. The key question, then, is, just how much running is required to achieve these goals? As we discussed earlier, not much. Great benefits can come from shorter, targeted runs. That's important because there are risks to running higher mileage.

With this in mind, my plan takes a new, economical approach to running: Instead of assuming that squeezing in an extra run is always a good idea, you're going to refrain from adding in that run unless you can articulate a specific benefit that would come from doing it. Any workout you do—whether it's running, strength training, or core work—should meet this same test. If you can't say what exactly an additional workout does for you, then you shouldn't do it. This is the essence of purposeful running.

Each of the workouts detailed in this book meet this test. Whether intended to trigger fat burning, improve speed, or strengthen certain muscle groups, each has a specific purpose.

A purposeful approach to training spells the end of those dull, slow slogs, where the miles seem endless and little aches and pains begin to add up, perhaps blossoming into a full-blown injury. It is not, however, an alternative to hard work. This program still calls for plenty of time spent in training. Only three days a week of it are for running, but those three days feature tough, targeted runs, implementing a form of high-intensity training. This approach provides more bang for the training buck, making each minute spent working out count more.

Consider this: A recent study showed that spending more than 60 minutes at constant intensity doesn't have much impact on mitochondrial density—that is, the body's ability to generate energy at the cellular level to perform work (Burgomaster et al. 2005; Gibala et al. 2006). Shorter, harder efforts, however, do increase mitochondrial density and also improve endurance performance. In 1996, Izumi Tabata from the National Institute of Fitness and Sports in Tokyo found that interval training of 20 seconds with a 10-second rest, repeated 8 times for a total of about 4 minutes of training, improved aerobic capacity by 14 percent, compared to 10 percent for an hour's worth of training (Jackson, Hickey, and Evans 2009).

Think about that. Four minutes of hard work was better than an hour's training. That's an astonishing finding not only for all athletes looking to improve but also for those of us who struggle to balance the time commitments of training with the needs of family and work.

3. **Cover all the bases**. When runners think about their bodies, they mostly think about their legs. It's not hard to understand why. These are the parts of the body that have to generate power and make contact with the ground, forming a churning drive chain that transfers power from the big muscles of the backside and hamstrings down to the feet. When that power is transferred to the ground, the result is forward motion. When something goes wrong, it's usually somewhere along this chain, whether in the muscles or ligaments that are directly involved in running or in the secondary muscles that stabilize and support the body throughout this motion.

   It would be a mistake, however, to think that running ends at the legs. In a lot of ways, that's where running actually begins. The abdominal and hip muscles, as well as the big muscles of the upper back, chest, shoulders, and arms, all work together to propel the body forward. My program spotlights these oft-overlooked areas by focusing on four modes of training that target them: core work, strength training, balance work, and drills.

4. **Know when to say when.** As runners, we all know that to be successful, we have to push ourselves to run, even when we sometimes don't feel like it. Often we're rewarded with a good run and the feeling afterward that we did the right thing.

   But sometimes the body isn't kidding; it really doesn't want to run. At those times, it's best to leave it be. The tough part, of course, is distinguishing one of these moments from the other and responding appropriately.

One tried and true indicator of fatigue is the resting heart rate (RHR). An elevated RHR is sign of a body that's stressed; it's working harder than usual to accomplish its basic task of simply keeping itself alive. Many elite runners monitor their RHR daily. Although an RHR that's a beat or two higher or lower per minute is not a cause for concern, an RHR that's 10 percent or more above the norm is a signal that something is wrong. When elite runners find themselves in that situation, many of them cancel their day's training plan. No argument, no debate, no guilt.

The first step in adopting this approach is to establish your RHR. Pick three consecutive days that will likely be routine, normal days, when you won't be out late or burning the midnight oil on a stressful work project. On each day, check your pulse immediately upon waking. At the end of the three days, find the average. That's your RHR.

Continue to check your pulse at that same time every day. That's important because your pulse will likely be different at other times of the day, so a spike in your heart rate would be normal and wouldn't reflect excess fatigue.

Another way to easily and effectively track your fatigue levels is by simply noting your mood, your enthusiasm for working out, and your performance. Anyone can have a bad run, but several bad runs in a row aren't good.

Sometimes bad days can add up without your noticing, which is one reason why it's important to keep a training log. By noting all the relevant data in a log—how you felt, how your workout went, what you ate, how well you slept—you will begin to notice trends and deviations. You can buy a training log, use one for free online, or make notes in a day planner or on a calendar. The important thing is to get in the habit of listening to and tracking what your body is trying to tell you.

Does all of this sound like too much work? Here's an even simpler test: How long does it take you to fall asleep at night? It should take about 10 minutes. Less than that indicates a high state of fatigue and sleep deprivation.

For many of us—myself included—logging enough hours of sleep each night is the greatest challenge. Failure to get enough sleep can undermine a training program because sleep is when the body releases human growth hormone (HGH), which not only heals the damage you inflicted on your muscles while training but also helps the body to resculpt itself to meet the new demands on it. Skip sleep, and your body cannot make these repairs and changes.

The real problem, however, is not that most runners can't spot fatigue. We all know when we're tired, sore, and cranky. It's that many runners feel that they dare not miss a workout. The guilt of skipping a planned run is simply too much for them. To these runners I pose this question: What do you think would be more fun and beneficial—to slog through a bad workout today and a bad workout tomorrow or to take today off and run the outsoles right off your shoes tomorrow?

Most people recognize what the right answer should be, but some of them still can't bring themselves to take the day off. That's a problem. I tell all of the athletes I coach that one of our prime rules is this: Do not be braver than you are smart. Working out when you should be resting is not being tough; it's being dumb. It's putting your health and the effectiveness of your program—and all the work you put into it—in jeopardy.

I once had a client who refused to take days off when I instructed him to do so, even after I explained how important it is to include recovery time in a workout schedule. The result was that he was fatigued on the days when I needed him to run faster. Not surprisingly, over the course of a full season he missed all of his race goals. We were both frustrated. I recognized that this was not a situation that would get any better until he could follow my advice. Until then, he would be essentially uncoachable.

Some athletes are dedicated enough to do the hard work but not dedicated enough to stop working when they should. You need to decide from the start which kind of athlete you're going to be.

5. **Make reasoned choices.** Every training program is, at its core, a balancing of opposing risks. On the one hand, there is the need to push the body hard enough to trigger the necessary adaptations that help

us achieve our goals. On the other hand, however, is the risk of injury that comes from pushing our bodies beyond the comfort zone.

Athletes who know their body's strengths and weaknesses can design a successful program because they know what works. Similarly, a good coach knows that there's no single right or wrong way to train; there's only what is effective and what is not for a particular runner. But even after a coach and an athlete follow a custom-designed program and achieve success, they may find that this same program does not work year after year. To keep racing at potential, an athlete needs to revisit the program choices she makes year after year.

This requires that the coach and athlete know their options—the tools at their disposal—and that they understand what these tools can and cannot do for them. When she gets it right, the athlete runs strong and injury-free. But when she gets it wrong, the athlete is stuck with uninspired racing or, worse, an injury-induced layoff.

And then, of course, there's the possibility that training and racing might not be an athlete's only priority. Often there's "that other stuff"—a spouse, kids, a career—that intrude on the perfect training plan. When that happens, compromises must be made. Workouts will be shortened, changed, or skipped altogether, and sometimes a whole week or more will be lost. There's no sense in pretending that this won't happen; the more realistic approach is to know in advance what to do when this occurs.

There are many options available to handle disruptions in training. Later in this book, we'll review specific adjustments you can make to accommodate your life without deviating from your training priorities. The key is this: Whatever you choose to do, you will be able to describe the risks and benefits of the change, why you chose it, and why it will help you stay on track.

That's the plan. In the chapters that follow, you'll find meat for these bones, including detailed half-marathon and marathon training schedules for intermediate, advanced, and competitive athletes, as well as detailed explanations of all core, strength, and balance exercises, as well as drills. We'll also discuss other issues, including proper running form, the advent of technology in training, racing strategies, and barefoot and minimalist shoe running.

By the end of this book, you will be a healthier runner. You will be able to take control of your training and use the ideas presented here to guide you in designing a plan that gets you to your goals. My hope and expectation are that, when followed faithfully, my program will make you the best runner you can be.

2

The Key Running Workouts

I ARGUED IN CHAPTER 1 OF THIS BOOK that the key to effective, injury-free training is to target the essential workouts in a training program and to avoid inflicting the unnecessary wear and tear on the body that result from running lots of miles that don't produce higher fitness. In this chapter, we'll review *what* those key workouts are, *why* we do them, and *how* to do them.

The four workouts you will be reading about here—the hill workout, the speed workout, the long run, and the tempo run (see Table 2.1)—will build strength, speed, and stamina, all without your getting bored and stale. In Chapter 3, we'll talk about crosstraining, which will round out your program.

Together, these are your Big Five—the workouts that form the foundation and structure of this program. Each serves a unique purpose in your workout plan. Together, they will help bring out the best in you. But you have to commit to doing them all. If you leave one of them out, you create a hole in your program. You might get away with that for a while, but in the end this omission will compromise the program and your results. So make up your mind right now and agree to take on the whole crew.

Before you begin the program, I highly recommend that you have your gait analyzed. See the sidebar on p.17 for an explanation as to why this preventive measure can potentially save you time and injury farther down the line in your training.

TABLE 2.1

RUN WORKOUTS

WORKOUT	PURPOSE	EFFORT LEVEL Rate of Perceived Exertion (RPE)*
HILL WORKOUT	Builds strength and speed; improves form	8–9
SPEED WORKOUT	Improves form; teaches pacing	8–9
LONG RUN	Builds an endurance base and running economy	6–7
TEMPO RUN	Trains the body to acclimate to a sustained intense effort; prepares the body for race day	8

*See Appendix B for RPE chart.

THE HILL WORKOUT
Why We Do It

Nothing builds strength and explosive speed like running *up*. Climbing up works the glutes, the hamstrings, and the calves—all the major muscle groups that are responsible for propelling you forward.

But what does hill running do that running on flat ground doesn't? Plenty. It builds power and explosive strength. Running up is really a series of short, one-legged squats. In a way, it's more akin to weight lifting and strength training than to running.

When you run up, you plant your foot and lift your body. That creates an adaptation stimulus that triggers the body to build denser muscle fibers, just like heavy lifting does, though at a lower intensity level. Because the huge loads of heavy squats and leg presses aren't involved in hill running, you are unlikely to add great muscle mass by running up. Nevertheless, the same type of explosive power can be generated.

Here's why: When you run up, you recruit muscle cells called fast-twitch fibers. You might have already heard about the difference between slow-twitch and fast-twitch muscle fibers. Slow-twitch fibers are the bread-and-butter of endurance athletes. These are the fibers that have the greatest density of mitochondria, which, as our high school biology teachers once

GAIT ANALYSIS

A knowledgeable and experienced expert can film a runner and review the results in real time and in slow motion, detecting inefficiencies or potential problem areas. See that hip sway? That's a gluteus medius issue. That bounce while running? That might stem from weak quadriceps, which cannot fully support the runner's weight on the landing phase of running. Gait analysis reveals these types of issues and points to the kinds of exercises that need to be done to correct the problem.

As a coach, I used to routinely recommend gait analysis for any of my athletes with an injury history. But eventually I realized that understanding the idiosyncrasies of each athlete's movements before he or she got injured would be an even better idea. Now before I work with any athlete, I require him or her to get checked out and filmed first before I design a training program. Doing so just makes sense.

To find a qualified expert to analyze your gait, start by asking people at your local running club or conduct a quick Web search. You can also ask at your local running store, but don't rely on its staff to perform a gait analysis, even if the store has a treadmill and a salesperson offers to take a look at your running style. Many running stores put their customers on a treadmill to help identify which shoes are appropriate for each runner and to give runners an opportunity to test ride a new pair of shoes. This can be helpful, but it isn't the same as getting a full analysis. Many running problems can be spotted only when an expert reviews the film in slow motion, which isn't something most running stores are prepared for or trained to do.

told us, are the powerhouses of the cell because they are the intracellular structures that convert fuel into energy. The more mitochondria you have, the greater volume of energy you can produce.

Endurance training creates a greater density of mitochondria in each cell. Increasing the density of mitochondria is one of the great benefits of long-distance running and the main reason for the improvements that we notice as we first begin to get fit.

What slow-twitch fibers don't do, however, is provide great speed. That's the realm of fast-twitch fibers. These fibers are thicker and produce more powerful contractions. When you think fast-twitch, think bodybuilder, sprinter, and weight lifter.

Each of us is born with a set ratio of fast-twitch to slow-twitch muscle fibers. In other words, your destiny as a long-distance runner or football lineman is basically set at birth. But if that's true, why are we concerned with training these fast-twitch fibers, and what use are they to us as long-distance runners?

The answer lies in a set of muscle fibers that are in the gray area between fast-twitch and slow-twitch. These fibers, known as Type IIB fibers, contain characteristics of both and respond to stimulus by adopting the characteristics of one type or the other. If you train them to be explosive, Type IIB fibers act that way, whereas if you train them to provide more steady energy, they'll do that, within the overall framework of your genetic predisposition.

For endurance runners, this is a great thing. It means that, although our potential as athletes is based in our genes, we might still have a great deal of control over our running destiny. A preponderance of slow-twitch fibers enables us to run for hour after hour, but with the proper training we can also develop speed and a finishing kick. The question, then, is, what can we do to push the fast-twitch fibers that we have, as well as our Type IIB fibers, to give us the speed we want?

The answer lies, partly, in running up. The stress of running up provides the right kind of stimulus to trigger improvements in those fast-twitch and Type IIB fibers—in much the same way that heavy weight lifting triggers those fibers, but without the same muscle-building response.

That's the long explanation of why we run hills. But here's another reason that we do it: Running hills and climbing stairs are easy on the body.

You're probably shaking your head right now, so I'll repeat myself: Hills and stairs are *easy*. Not on your muscles and lungs, of course—to them, running up can be murderous. But to the knees, ankles, hips, and vertebrae, running up is a holiday.

That's because running up involves very little falling. Think about it: With every step, you lift your leg and place it at a point higher than it was where it started. Even though you still have to step down to meet the ground, the impact stresses are lower than they would be if you were running on even ground because that step down is shorter than would otherwise be the case.

Once that foot is planted, that leg is responsible not only for propelling the body forward but also for pushing your entire body weight *up*. Because that push up occurs when the foot is planted, there are no significant impact forces at play at all during that phase of the running motion. Put this all together, and you have a great, exhausting, and *productive* workout that doesn't inflict any excessive wear and tear on your body.

We can look at this dynamic another way by analyzing downhill running. That kind of workout does the opposite, creating a footfall that is *greater* than that found on flat-ground running. Each step involves the foot dropping below its starting point, creating a greater impact shock than would occur on flat-ground running. That shock has to be absorbed not only by the muscles—primarily the quadriceps in the front of the legs—but also by the joints, especially the knees, hips, and spine. When we recall that flat-ground running involves impact forces of up to four times your body weight on each step, we can appreciate how much more pounding downhill running entails.

With all that in mind, we can easily see why so many runners prefer running uphill than down. Uphill might be hard, but downhill *hurts*. (Of course, if your target race involves a lot of downhill running, you'll have to practice this in training to acclimate the body for what you'll be asking it to do. We will talk more about downhill running in Chapter 6.)

But as the late-night TV hucksters say, "Wait! There's more!" As an extra bonus, the uphill running helps improve running form and economy, forcing athletes to shorten their stride and increase their leg turnover. That's because running uphill makes it impossible to commit one of the cardinal sins of running: overstriding.

Planting your foot too far in front of your body forces you to land on your heel, which is the one part of your foot that is least prepared to handle any impact force. Your body would much prefer to land midfoot. The midfoot landing puts stress on the arch, which can respond by flattening and flexing to absorb the impact. The heel doesn't flatten or flex. It just takes the hit, or it breaks.

Another fault of overstriding is that it creates backward forces that must be overcome, wasting energy that could be better spent moving forward. This is basic Newtonian physics: Every action creates an equal and opposite reaction. Plant your foot in front of your body, and the opposite reaction generated is a backward force. The farther in front you plant your foot, the greater the backward push generated. But if you plant your foot directly below you, there's no backward push; all your energy can be spent on forward motion from this neutral starting point.

This is why many of the world's best runners, at distances from 100-meter sprints to 100-mile ultramarathons, are midfoot strikers. This efficiency enables them both to avoid placing undue stress on their feet and to conserve precious energy.

Now that I've (hopefully) convinced you of the benefits of uphill running and the dangers of downhill running, you might expect me to say that you should avoid downhill running at all costs. Not so. There's a time and place to work on downhill running, and we'll get to that later when discussing strategies for specific racecourses. But for now, up is the way to go.

How to Do It

There are two issues that have to be resolved when setting up a hill workout: knowing what constitutes proper form and deciding how much hill is necessary.

We already started on the ground level (literally) by discussing foot strike and leg turnover when running hills. Moving on up the chain, you should lean forward slightly from the ankles, which will help generate momentum by emphasizing the falling-forward phase of running. But do *not* bend at the waist, as tempting as this might be on steep hills. This places lots of stress on the lower back, which is exactly the kind of outcome that we're trying to avoid.

Moving upward, you should keep your back straight and your elbows bent while swinging your arms smoothly from your shoulders. Many runners twist their bodies and either allow their hands to cross past their midlines or hold their arms close to their bodies as they rotate their trunks. Both of these running styles stress the lower back by introducing unnecessary rotation.

HOW TO AVOID OVERSTRIDING

How do you know if you're overstriding and heel striking? You could have someone film you running and then check your foot plant, but there's an easier way: Count steps.

Research has shown that the best runners, at all distances, take approximately 180 steps per minute (Pfitzinger 2006). That's counting each step, both left and right. The differences in their speeds have to do with the power they generate with each step, but their basic mechanics are the same. If you're taking that many steps, it's very unlikely that you're overstriding.

Most of us, however, take something on the order of 160 steps per minute. This means not only that we may be heel striking but also that we're missing up to twenty opportunities each minute to push off and generate forward motion. Add that up in a half-marathon or marathon, and that could be the difference between a PR and just another day on the roads—all at the same energy expenditure level.

How can you increase your leg turnover and hit 180? Practice. Count steps. Set a small, handheld electronic metronome at 180 beats per minute, and work on matching your foot strike to it. Eventually, you'll have trained your body to run at this new cadence.

And run hills. When you run uphill, you naturally have to shorten your stride length. Once this is imprinted on your neural system, it should be easier to replicate on the flats and downhills.

Failure to swing the arms from the shoulders also squanders the opportunity for them to generate momentum and help pull your body up the hill. We've all experienced this phenomenon, even if we haven't been consciously aware of it: The harder and faster we swing our arms, the more likely we are to swing our legs to match. That's because the arms and legs work in tandem, swinging in opposition (left leg–right arm, right arm–left leg), rotating on the central axis of the body in order to maintain balance. Speed up one part of this chain of motion, and the other parts will pretty much follow along. To get the most out of your arm swing, put more effort on the back swing than the front swing, focusing on pushing your elbows back.

Don't ignore the front swing, however; that should be strong, too. Your elbows should stay bent through the entire motion at about a 75-degree angle, which is pretty tight. On the downstroke, your hand should be near the bottom of your ribs; on the upstroke, your hand should come up just below jaw level.

Your hands should be relaxed. Too many runners waste energy by clenching their hands tightly as they run. A better idea would be to direct all of your energy to the muscles that are moving you forward, while keeping everything else as relaxed as possible. To achieve this, imagine that you're carrying a single potato chip to a starving friend. You don't want to crush it or lose any of it, so it has to be held firmly but very gently.

The last item on your form checklist is your head position. You should run tall, looking straight ahead. Avoid looking down at your feet, even if looking up fills you with dread. We all have a tendency to move in the direction we're looking, so if you look down, you're likely to start bending over as well. Instead, pick a spot up ahead and focus on it like a laser. A sign, tree, or streetlight works well. Just aim for that landmark, and you'll get there quicker than you might think.

Some coaches give very particular instructions for their hill work, recommending such things as a 9 percent incline for 100 meters. I've never met anyone who could tell me with any confidence or authority what those numbers look like in real life. And what if you can't find any hills that match those precise numbers?

Instead of aiming for that kind of precision, we're going to go with an effort-based approach, centered on your own preferences. And then we'll add in some variety to keep the whole thing interesting and to challenge your body in different ways.

First, let's talk about the effort. To make this workout effective, you have to make it intense. A gentle incline won't do the job; you need a hill that will take just about everything you have to reach its top. You could use a heart rate monitor to measure your effort and aim to get your heart rate up to 80–85 percent of your maximum heart rate (MHR).

But this assumes that you know your MHR. The only sure way to find your true maximum heart rate is to have a stress test administered in a clinical setting on a regular basis. For most of us, this isn't a feasible option, so exercise physiologists have calculated a number of formulas that can be used to approximate the MHR, but these can be significantly off the mark.

The best approach turns out to be the easiest: I recommend using the rate of perceived exertion (RPE), which is based on your own perception of how hard you're working. Most people are pretty good at gauging their own effort levels with a surprisingly high amount of precision. If your workout feels easy, hard, or hardest, it probably is, and no expensive gadget or complicated testing is required to help you understand that.

In practice, we use the RPE this way: Imagine a scale of 1 to 10, with 1 being sleepwalking and 10 being a gasping, red-faced, all-out effort. All of your endurance and speed workouts will fall somewhere between 6 and 9 on this scale. As we discuss the workouts that you'll be doing, we'll refer to this scale to understand what your effort level should be. (See Appendix B for further explanation of RPE.)

With all that in mind, let's get back to our hill running. On a scale of 1 to 10, with 10 being the hardest, conquering the hill should have put you somewhere in the 8 to 9 range. Not dead on your feet, but close.

Second, let's decide what kind of hills you like to run. Some athletes prefer regularity and exactitude. For these athletes, it's important to run repeats of the same hill, timing each trip up. I've got nothing against that; it's an effective, intense workout. If that sounds like your kind of workout, find a good local hill and make that your proving ground.

As for me, I prefer changing scenery and varying terrain. If this sounds more like you, too, then try this: Make a list of the toughest hills in town, and map out different loops that incorporate four, five, and six of them. These will be your workouts.

Traditionally, hill running is done once a week, early in a running season, to build strength in anticipation of track work. Once track season begins and athletes start working directly on improving speed, structured hill running generally ceases.

This is a sensible, reasoned progression, and I have no problem with it. But there are other approaches that would also work well. You could continue to do hill repeats once a week as part of your speed workout. This makes for an exhausting, but effective, workout. Or you could alternate between track work and hill work. Finally, you could design your long runs to include some hills. This can serve to not only bring some variation to your long run but also to help prepare you for your target race if you could map out a route that mimics the race's elevation profile.

Alternatives

If you live in Texas or Florida, you're probably shaking your head right now because apart from a few overpasses, there might not be one hill within 50 miles, let alone six of them. Or what if a fierce winter storm rolls into your town and you can't run your favorite hill. What do you do then?

You're not off the hook; you just need to be creative. Any underground parking ramp will fill in nicely—just ignore the confused looks from drivers or staff, and watch for oncoming traffic.

Stairs provide the same benefits as hill running, but in a precise, controlled environment. A stairwell in a 10-story or higher building is perfect, but be sure to check with building security to make sure that the doors open from the inside and that you are allowed to be in the stairwell. You don't want to be stuck in a stairwell that's locked because of security concerns.

Once inside, run up hard, taking two steps at a time, and come back down slowly, using that time for recovery. Avoid using the handrails because that lightens the load on your legs and prevents them from getting the workout they need.

Whatever location you plan to use, make hills a staple of your workout routine.

THE SPEED WORKOUT
Why We Do It

Climbing hills builds strength, as we just discussed. But if you want to become a faster runner, you have to train to run fast. Whether you call these speed workouts, as I do here, interval training, or running track, we're talking about the same thing: running short distances repeatedly at fast speeds, punctuated with slow recovery jogs that never seem to last long enough.

If you were ever a member of your high school track team, or have run track workouts with a group as an adult recreational athlete, then you know what track workouts look like: They're repeats of set distances run at specific speeds, punctuated with short, easy recovery intervals. The repeats are run hard, and the recovery intervals are slow jogs.

The first question we might ask is, why break up the run this way? The answer is that, even though running hard is great for building speed, running hard also raises the risk of getting injured. It puts stress on the joints and ligaments and causes microtears to the muscles used. This is all necessary because the body will react by improving all those structures to handle running hard, but to run hard is to tread on a razor's edge; even just a little too much can result in more stress than the body can easily handle and repair. The result? An injury that can set you back days or weeks.

In a race, that's a risk we're usually willing to take, having, we hope, prepared properly for a near maximal effort. But long-distance runners generally don't race hard every week because a half- or full marathon can require recovery time ranging from several weeks to a month of easy running. With that in mind, how could we possibly plan to run hard every week in training without getting hurt?

The answer lies in those recovery intervals. By breaking down the hard running into more manageable chunks and giving the body a little rest time between each, we can moderate the stress involved and spoon-feed hard running to our bodies.

The next question might be, why do these workouts have to be so precise? As you may have guessed from our discussion on hill running, I like to keep the structure of my workouts a little loose when I can and just enjoy the journey of running as much as possible. But for a speed workout, we have to act like scientists, creating data that we can effectively compare from week to week, monitoring our progress and making adjustments as we go. Only then can we make the incremental improvements that add up to big gains.

Here's how it works. Long-distance running is aerobic. That means the body needs oxygen to metabolize the fuel it uses to run for long periods of time. That fuel is glycogen, a form of sugar that's found in the bloodstream and stored in the liver. In contrast, short bursts of activity mostly use a different fuel, which can be processed by the body without oxygen. That's why very short, intense bursts of exercise, like power lifting, are called anaerobic. As distance runners, we operate mostly in the aerobic zone.

The breakpoint between aerobic and anaerobic running is referred to as the lactic threshold (also sometimes referred to as the anaerobic threshold). Lactic acid is the byproduct of the body's fuel metabolism. The lactic threshold marks the point at which the body is working so hard that it begins to build up more lactic acid than it can easily clear. The result is that familiar burning feeling we get when we run too fast for too long.

Highly trained athletes have acclimated their bodies to not only clearing lactic acid but also rechanneling it back for further metabolism. In other words, to use as fuel. The higher the lactic threshold is, the higher the level of intense exercise that our bodies can tolerate. In effect, then, the lactic threshold sets the upper limit for how fast we can go when we run.

Want to run faster? Then raise your lactic threshold. To do this, you need to produce a training effect that will result in an elevation of the body's ability to clear lactic acid.

To some degree, hill running accomplishes this because running hills builds strength in the fast-twitch muscle fibers, which are also responsible for generating speed. But hill running doesn't acclimate the body to a faster running cadence. Put simply, to be a faster runner, you have to practice running fast. After all the formulas and workouts are proposed and analyzed, it still all comes down to that simple proposition.

There might be another explanation, too, for what happens when we run fast. Dr. Tim Noakes of the University of Cape Town in South Africa, a leading expert in the field of exercise science, has proposed the existence of a different adaptation that results from speed work (Noakes 2003). Dr. Noakes thinks that the upper limit of our speed is set not by our muscles but by our minds.

Dr. Noakes analyzed the body measurements of athletes who had run to exhaustion, and he discovered that there was no measurable physiological basis that would explain why these athletes found their bodies shutting down. Their core temperature hadn't risen dangerously high, and their blood sugar was still at acceptable levels. Why, then, had their performance started to decline?

Or consider this puzzle: When we're running hard and we stop for a few moments to get some water or to use the restroom, why is it so hard to get started again? It can't be that our bodies have cooled down; that doesn't occur in just a minute or two. What causes that sudden roadblock in our running?

Dr. Noakes thinks he has the answer to both questions: that something in the autonomic part of our brains is calling the shots. He theorizes that this structure monitors our physical activity and acts to protect us from our own recklessness. It accomplishes this by shutting down whenever it perceives a threat to the body's overall health. Dr. Noakes terms this structure, rather ominously, "the Central Governor."

In support of his theory, Dr. Noakes references those moments when runners inexplicably slow down; he also tracks the century-long progress of various track and field world records. Why, he asks, have these records dropped incrementally rather than just plummeting to their final position?

Because each distance has been run by a large group of highly trained athletes over time, the limits of human performance should have theoretically been reached easily within a generation or two. Even when technological breakthroughs such as improved gear, tracks, and (illegal) performance-enhancing drugs are factored in, our final limitations should have been hit pretty quickly. And yet the world records in distances from the 200 meters to the marathon creep down just second by second over the years. Why?

Again, Dr. Noakes points to the Central Governor. He assumes, reasonably enough, that athletes who take aim at world records think of breaking them, but not by leaps and bounds. This creates a target only for a certain effort level, even if a greater effort might actually be attainable. In other words, when the limits imposed by the Central Governor are combined with the limited expectations of athletes, the result is a field of athletes who are only prepared to push the limits of their disciplines forward bit by bit.

Dr. Noakes doesn't believe that it has to be this way. If an athlete were convinced that he or she could better the world record by a huge amount— say, breaking the 2-hour barrier in the marathon—perhaps that athlete would train accordingly and prepare the brain for that kind of grueling effort.

This is an intriguing and revolutionary concept. If true, it means that the point of training is only partly to prepare the body to run fast. The other, perhaps more important function of training is to satisfy the brain that the body won't blow up if we push it hard.

But in the end, does all this really even matter? To theorists and scientists, sure, but for coaches and athletes, the bottom line is still this: Training for a great race performance requires performing repeats of hard running.

But there's another benefit of running intervals, apart from simply gaining speed. As we run repeats, we begin to associate a given effort level with a particular speed. This develops in us the ability to monitor our pace, which is a crucial skill for effective racing.

The best practical example of this was a runner I knew from a local track. One evening we decided to dovetail our workouts, which were going to be a series of 400-meter repeats. My friend announced that she intended to run each at about 1 minute 13 seconds, but I noticed that she wasn't wearing a running watch. Nevertheless, we began our workout. I silently noted the time it took us to complete each lap. Sure enough, she churned out each one within a second or two of her goal.

I walked away from this workout amazed at my friend's ability to connect her effort with her internal clock. But really, this is a skill that most of us already possess, without even being consciously aware of it—when we drive.

Most people have a fairly accurate sense of how fast they're driving, even without looking down at the speedometer. That's because we subconsciously notice how quickly we pass light posts, parked cars, and other stationary objects. After a while, we develop an ability to process all of these cues and turn it into a rough estimate of our speed.

Running track develops this same ability. The trick is to use this skill on race day when adrenaline can overwhelm our rational thinking and encourage us to run faster than we should. We'll return to that problem in Chapter 6.

How to Do It

Think of a track as a blank canvas. The size and shape of the canvas set the outside parameters, but within that space each artist has almost unlimited freedom to do what she wishes.

Track workouts are the same way. A standard track is 400 meters around—just about a quarter mile. But the workouts that can be done on them can be structured to build sprinting speed, middle-distance speed, or long-distance speed. The key is to know what effort levels should be targeted for each type of workout and what distances and progressions are optimal for each respective race goal.

As with any program where there are a great many options available, there are many differences of opinion on what works best for each athlete. An old coaching joke is that if you throw two coaches into a room, they'll come out with three different training plans. There's a lot of truth to that. But that's because there's no single workout that works equally for each athlete or that even works the same for each athlete from season to season. The key is not to look for the "perfect" workout but to know the options that are available and how to choose among them.

At the most basic level, there are three variables at play in designing a track workout: speed, distance, and recovery time. Every track workout needs to nail down numbers for each of these variables. Once you are sufficiently warmed up—and we'll review that process in just a moment—your workout will consist of running specific distances at specific paces, with specific easy-jog recovery times between each hard effort. Generally, the shorter the distance and the faster the speed, the longer the recovery time. The reason for this is to minimize the risk of injury by carefully managing the stress put on your body. Come race day, you'll be pushing all these variables as hard as you can, as you run long and fast without recovery time. But that kind of effort is reserved for race day. When you review the training programs in Chapter 9, you'll see how these variables are managed in our workouts.

SPEED AND EFFORT

For speed, the number will be based on your finishing times at various race distances during the preceding 12 months. This both customizes your workout to your current fitness and provides an ongoing method for adjusting your track times as you get faster. Refer to Table 2.2 to see how speed work distances and race paces match up. (For details on figuring out your pace based on various distances, see Appendix A.)

If you haven't raced any or some of those distances within 12 months, or ever, you can go by your RPE, which we discussed when reviewing hill running. The shorter the repeat distance, the higher you should be on the RPE scale.

Having trouble identifying your RPE? You can match these against your race pace if you've run races of various distances over the preceding year. That's because when you run shorter distances, you can run at a higher intensity at a faster pace. Your range of race times over various distances will correlate roughly to various RPE rates, so if you know one, you can figure out the other.

See Table 2.2 to find out how to match your RPE to your race pace, recovery time, and interval workout distance. We'll rely on race paces for a few of the most popular race distances: the 5K, 10K, and half-marathon.

Keep in mind that you should be pacing your workout so that your last repeat is your fastest. If you find that you're slowing down as you run, stop your workout—you've burned yourself out, and any further running may cause injury. It takes discipline to run hard while running controlled, but once mastered, it's an invaluable tool to have in your racing arsenal.

THE WARM-UP

As a general rule, most track workouts traditionally consist of 3 to 4 miles of speed, punctuated by another mile of recovery, broken up into small bites for

TABLE 2.2
PACING FOR SPEED WORK

DISTANCE	RPE	RACE PACE	RECOVERY INTERVAL
50–100 m	9	5K minus 1 min.	10 sec.
200 m	9	5K minus 30 sec.	100 m
400 m	8–9	5K	200 m
800 m	8	10K	200 m
1,600 m	8	HALF-MARATHON	400 m

each repeat. Combined with a mile warm-up and a mile cooldown, the entire workout usually covers a total of about 6–7 miles.

Except when it doesn't. On occasion, it's good practice to push beyond the usual limits. In the great novel *Once a Runner*, author John L. Parker Jr. describes a monumental workout performed by the main character, an aspiring Olympic miler. It begins with a set of 20 repeats of 400 meters. To his dismay, his coach immediately calls for a second set of 20 repeats of 400 meters. And then, you guessed it: a final set of 20 times 400 meters. All together, that's 60 times 400 meters, or roughly 12.5 miles of gut-busting speed work.

In the novel, the miler has, by the end of the workout, run himself dangerously close to total collapse and has to be carried to his room by his coach. The point was to show the runner how far he could really push himself and how much suffering he could really endure.

We won't be doing any workouts like those here, but some of these workouts will still test your resolve and force you to confront your inner demons. Don't be afraid to push yourself.

Before running fast, however, you have to ease your body into it by effectively warming it up. First, run an easy warm-up mile on the track. This will increase blood flow to working muscles, increase muscle and ligament pliability, and force lubricating fluid into creaky joints.

Next, pick a short stretch of track—50 meters or so—to run drills alternately as you go down and back (see p.33 for the sidebar on running drills). You might feel silly when you do them, but they're the same drills used by elite pro athletes, Olympians, high school and college track teams, and thousands of runners like you, all hoping to squeeze out a little more speed from their legs. These drills will effectively prepare specific muscles in the body for what you're about to ask them to do.

The question, then, is *when* to do them. Drills are easiest to schedule; there are only six drills in our program, and each one takes about a minute. Traditionally, drills are incorporated into the weekly speed work routine as part of the warm-up. Some people also do them as part of the cooldown after a run. We'll do both, incorporating drills into two of our three weekly runs, before the speed work and after the tempo run.

At the track, the order that you'll follow in your workout will be;

- easy warm-up
- drills
- striders
- workout
- cooldown

THE WORKOUTS

20 × 50 or 100 meters with a 10-second recovery. These are sprints run near the body's limit—a 9 out of 10 on the RPE scale. This is a fast, brutal workout that builds quick leg turnover, passing speed, and a finishing kick. This workout will certainly teach you about suffering, which is a valuable bit of self-knowledge to have when you hit a rough patch during a race (and, if we believe the Central Governor theory, an indispensible tool in convincing the brain that hard running isn't harmful).

Here's where the difference between sprinters and long-distance runners is most apparent: Sprinters might run just a handful of these and take 5 to 10 minutes between repeats, letting their bodies enjoy full recovery. But distance runners can't enjoy this luxury because their races can last hours, not just seconds.

20 × 200 or 400 meters with a 2-minute recovery. This is another speed workout that trains the mind as much as the body. It's a brutal workout but once completed, leads to soaring confidence. If you can get through this, there's nothing to fear in a race. And the bright side is that the repeats are so quick and the recoveries so short that there's simply not a lot of time to think about how miserable you feel and how much you wish you had stayed home instead. But once the workout is over, there's hardly a better feeling in the world.

Similar to the 50- or 100-meter sprints, this workout builds strong finishing speed. When you are in sight of the finish line at the end of your goal race and the seconds are ticking away on your new PR, you'll be able to find a new gear to shift into to hit that finish line, courtesy of this workout.

6–8 × 800 meters with a 3-minute recovery. This workout is the pack mule of running, an all-purpose workout that effectively builds speed for

RUNNING DRILLS

BUTT KICKS. These are exactly what they sound like: You kick up your heels as you run, aiming to nail your own backside with your heels (Fig. 2.1). The key is not to rush the running; we are aiming to warm up the hamstring muscles of the back of the upper leg, so the speed of forward motion isn't at all important.

SOCCER KICKS. This drill requires you to stay on your toes and keep your knees locked out as much as possible as you run the 50 meters stiff-legged (Fig. 2.2). Do not exaggerate your step or hyperextend your legs. The point of this drill is not to increase flexibility; it's about improving muscle strength and warming up the hip flexor muscles.

HIGH STEPS. Run the next segment by lifting your knees as high as you can with each step (Fig. 2.3). The steps should be very rapid; imagine that you're running on hot coals, and swing your arms quickly to set the pace. This drill will prepare the hip flexor muscles on the front of the hips, as well as the calf muscles used during the push-off phase of running. Don't race down the track with this drill either.

2.1

2.2

2.3

CONTINUED

CONTINUED

HIGH SKIPS. Skip just like you did as a kid, taking a short hop before each step. For this drill, however, swing your arms forcefully and try to get as high in the air as possible (Fig. 2.4).

2.4

If you never skipped as a kid—and I see this quite frequently—you might find it tough at first to get your body to cooperate. Don't get discouraged; your body will get the hang of it soon enough. Remember that the arm that's supposed to swing is on the opposite side from the leg that's supposed to move forward. If you really have difficulty coordinating this, you might find it helpful to first get the legs moving before getting the arms involved.

AGILITY DRILL. This drill is the only one that requires you to run out and back because the muscles used going in one direction are different from the muscles used on the return trip. For those of you who are familiar with aerobics classes, this drill mimics the grapevine move. Facing sideways in a lane, step sideways as fast as possible, stepping first in front of your other leg and then behind it, as you keep you upper body as still as possible (Fig. 2.5).

2.5

This is what it should look like: Bring your left leg across in front, step out next with your right leg, and then step across behind with your left leg. Repeat, crossing in front, then behind, then in front, and behind.

The muscles used in this movement include the stabilizers of the inner and outer hip. These muscles, also known, respectively as the adductors and abductors, are crucial to maintaining proper form while running. Weakness in this area is responsible for many of the injuries commonly experienced by runners. In Chapters 4 and 5, we'll learn more exercises we can do to keep these muscles strong.

STRIDERS. The drills so far have focused on individual muscle groups, warming them up and getting them ready to work hard. Once this is accomplished, your body is ready to run fast. All that's missing is a transition from isolationist-type movements, in which specific muscles are targeted, to regular running at high intensity. This drill is that bridge. It's not part of the actual speed workout because it's not run fast enough or far enough to trigger an adaptation response, but it involves a faster, more energetic leg turnover than a simple warm-up jog, so it serves as the final preparation for fast running.

Striders are to be run fast, but speed is not the point. When running striders, you should be analyzing your form. Are your elbows bent, and are you swinging your arms from your shoulder instead of rotating your body? Are you running tall and keeping your head up, with your eyes focused on a distant point?

To get an idea of how fast to run striders, try this imagery: Picture yourself heading to a bus stop. You can see that down the block the bus you need to be on is already at your stop, picking up passengers. There are still a few people on line to board, but once they're on the bus, it will leave. You need to hurry and get there, but you're not yet in a panic. Run with determination, but not at breakneck speed.

race distances ranging from the 5K to the marathon. It's short enough to allow you to run at a very fast pace, yet long enough to work outside the purely anaerobic zone.

3–6 × 1,600 meters with a 3-minute recovery. This is the bread and butter of half-marathoners and full marathoners. It requires not just speed and endurance but also a higher level of mental toughness.

The third of the four laps that comprise a 1,600-meter repeat might be the toughest in all of running. The first lap is all energy and optimism. The second lap marks only the onset of fatigue, still in its infancy. The fourth, final lap is run with the knowledge that the end of the agony is only moments away. But that third lap has no friends; fatigue has made a home in the legs, and the end of the repeat feels like it may never come. And when that third lap is completed, there's still one more lap to go.

This is where true mental toughness is born—the ability to push through fatigue and doubt when the race is little more than half over and you know for certain that the remaining miles will be long and difficult. But when your race seems unwinnable, remember the way you toughed it out on those seemingly endless mile repeats at the track and quiet those doubts.

Stepladder. Variety is the spice of life, as the saying goes, and that definitely applies to the track. Some people might enjoy running the track, but for most of us it's a means to an end. We want speed and are willing to work for it, but running loop after loop on a nearly featureless circuit can often feel, well, mind-numbing. Some variety—*any* variety—can feel like finding an ice-cold thermos on a desert island.

That's what a stepladder workout can feel like. Its structure is quite simple: You progress from short-distance repeats up to a long repeat, adding distance incrementally, and then work your way back down. A typical stepladder workout might be 400-600-800-1,200-800-600-400, with a 400-meter/ 3-minute recovery between each, but there is a nearly endless supply of possible combinations. You could do a double stepladder, building up twice, or build up by larger increments.

Whatever you choose, you'll probably find it interesting to shift into different paces as you run different distances. The shorter the interval distance, the faster the pace should be. In general, you could run your 100 and 200 meter intervals at your mile pace, 400 meters at your 5K pace, and 800 meters and mile repeats at 10K pace. Refer to Appendix A if you have questions about figuring out your pace. All the effort you spend figuring out this workout and getting through the intervals will pay off when you feel that unexpected speed and strength when you drop back down to the last short, fast repeat at the end of the workout.

Alternatives

Track workouts are usually done in groups, and that's for a reason. Groups of runners will tend to rise to the highest common denominator, as competitive streaks get ignited and people get swept up in the energy. Different people may take the lead from week to week, but when a group is running together, almost everyone ends up having a better workout than any of them would have had alone.

Sometimes, however, running with a group is just not an option. Perhaps there's no organized track workout in your neighborhood, or you're traveling. Or even if you have a group, perhaps extreme weather has made running on a track unsafe. In these cases, it's important to know what other options you might have.

One option is the treadmill. You will probably wince when you read that. But let me explain. And keep an open mind.

I've yet to meet a runner who admits to enjoying a treadmill run. I can understand and accept that. As runners, we generally love to be outdoors. Running track isn't as much fun as running trails and bike paths, but it still beats running in place indoors. I can't change that. But there are reasons that running on a treadmill is a good alternative.

First, it's reliable. No matter the conditions outside, it will be there for you. If the sky is dark and foreboding, or the weather wet and nasty, it's still safe and comfortable indoors.

Second, the treadmill is consistent. You know exactly what pace you are running moment to moment, and you can ensure that your last repeat is your fastest because all you have to do is set the monitor and try to keep up.

Of course, I know that there is a seemingly endless debate about whether treadmill running can really be as effective as running on roads because there is no wind resistance while you are running on a treadmill and the road is fed to you as you run.

All that may be true. But for us, for the most part, it's irrelevant. Even though exercise physiologists might worry about slight differences, it's not something that should really concern us because a fast pace on the treadmill will still create an adequate adaptation response.

Consider Christine Clark, the poster girl of treadmill running. In 2000, she became the sole American female qualifier for the Sydney Olympics—

after having done most of her training on a treadmill. Clark was living in Anchorage, Alaska, at the time, and in the winter in Alaska treadmill running became her only option. She made the most of it, and so can you. Just set the treadmill at a 1 percent incline to compensate slightly for the differences and get going.

There are a few things you can do to make a treadmill workout more tolerable. Music and television are always good distractions, but my fear when running speed workouts on a treadmill is forgetting how many repeats I've already done. That involves the related problem of having my IQ drop in direct proportion to the length and difficulty of my workout. Math was never a strong suit of mine anyway, but while running, my competency drops down to frighteningly low levels. For me, there's always the lurking danger that I'll simply forget where in the workout I am.

That's why I invented the "penny method." Add up the total number of repeats you're scheduled to run, and then gather up that same number of pennies. Put them in the water bottle holder on your treadmill console, and begin the workout. After each repeat, drop a penny into another cup holder, if there is one, or simply toss it on the floor. When you're out of pennies, you're done with your speed work.

THE LONG RUN
Why We Do It

Earlier in this chapter, we discussed the different fuel paths used by the body to energize its movements—the aerobic and anaerobic systems—and then went on to talk about some speed-building workouts. But the defining characteristic of long-distance runners is the ability to, well, run long distances.

Whether running a half- or a full marathon, a long-distance runner will be out on the roads for well over an hour. To accomplish this, we have to do some specialized training, meaning that we have to spend time putting in long miles in the road. The question for us, as always, is how to strike a balance between getting all the training that we need and not putting more stress on our bodies than is absolutely necessary.

Many people believe that the long run is necessary in order to build up the muscles used in running. That's only partly true. The real benefit of the long run is in teaching the body to rely less on glycogen—that is, blood sugar—and more on the most abundant fuel supply: fat. Even the thinnest marathoner has more than enough fat to fuel many hours of exercise, and here's why: As we discussed in Chapter 1, fat is more than twice as calorie dense as carbohydrates and protein. Fat is also more densely packed into the body than other fuels. Carbohydrates need water in order to be stored by the body—which is why many people feel bloated after a big pasta dinner—but fats do not, making them easier to store.

It would seem, then, that fat would be the body's fuel of choice because it's readily available and packed with energy. But that's not the case. The process used to turn fat into energy is more complicated than it is for carbs or protein. Our bodies naturally tend to go along the path of least resistance, and for fuel, that means carbs stored in the body as sugar. The body warehouses sugar in muscle cells, in the bloodstream, and mostly in the liver, but unfortunately, it doesn't keep very much on hand—only enough to fuel about two hours' worth of exercise.

Two hours isn't a very long time. You could easily fit a short race into that span, like a 5K, but not necessarily a longer race, like a half- or full marathon. Sugar alone won't get you to the finish line in those races. In those cases, the body will eat up all its stored sugar and then simply begin to shut down.

This is the infamous wall that we mentioned earlier. If you've never experienced hitting the wall yourself, let me tell you, it's not much fun. It feels as though someone has suddenly disconnected your power cord. When it happened to me late in one unfortunate marathon, I found myself slowing down within a few minutes from a fast run to a shuffle. It's a frustrating and humbling experience.

Or when faced with a fuel shortage, the body could choose to do something even worse: It could begin to cannibalize itself. Protein is found everywhere in the body, especially in the skeletal muscles we use to accomplish all voluntary movement, like running. Protein contains four calories per gram, just like carbs, which makes it an inferior fuel choice to fat in the long run. Protein is also harder for the body to metabolize than sugar. Despite all this, the body still may choose to use protein as fuel when the sugar runs out.

I learned this firsthand once, the hard way. I had just finished running the San Francisco Marathon and met up with a friend who had also just finished the race. We had made arrangements to have some other friends pick us up, but once we got inside their car, I became aware of my strong body odor. It wasn't just the stink of old sweat, however; I reeked of *ammonia*.

No one said anything, but it was bad. Really bad. I had no idea why this was happening to me, but I was mortified. After a few minutes, I couldn't take the polite silence any longer. I apologized for my stink and admitted that I had no idea what was going on.

It was only later that I learned that ammonia is a byproduct of protein metabolism (Graham et al. 1995). During the race, my body had run out of glycogen and had decided to start eating itself. I was probably lucky that the race ended at 26.2 miles.

The key to successful long-distance running, then, is to convince the body to go easy on the sugar and to start eating fat as soon as possible. Luckily, that's not a very complicated thing to do; whenever we engage in progressively longer bouts of aerobic exercise lasting more than an hour, we coax the body into dipping into its fat stores. It's a simple formula: Do the hard work; avoid the wall. Or to put it another way: When someone bonks late in a race, it's a very public admission that he failed to do his homework.

Most distance runners already know this. The problem is that their bodies just can't hold up to the training they know they have to do to avoid bonking. It's a damned-if-you-do-damned-if-you-don't dilemma: suffer an injury in training or suffer collapse in the race. Having read this far, you know that the point of this book is to break away from that kind of limited, all-or-nothing choice.

We'll soon be talking about the nonrunning elements of your training plan that will keep you strong and protect you from injury, but there's still no getting around the basic rule that in order to be a long distance runner, you have to run long.

How to Do It

The first and most important rule of the long run is to not push the pace. Running long is challenging enough for the body without the extra stress of speed. Elite runners aim to do their long runs at about 60 to 90 seconds slower per mile than their race pace. You should, too. There's a time and place in our program for building speed, but this isn't it.

The second and almost equally important rule of the long run is to build up gradually. Your body can adapt to a wide variety of challenges if you give it enough time. A solid rule of thumb in coaching is to recommend an increase of no more than 10 percent from week to week for both the long run and total mileage.

My own coaching approach is to be more flexible than that, especially where a runner already has years of running and racing experience. But still, I generally recommend adding no more than 2 miles at a time to the long run.

The long run isn't really a complicated thing. As long as you stay in an easy zone—about a 6 on the RPE scale—and stay fueled and hydrated as you would in a race, all should be well. But as fatigue sets in, running form often suffers. Shoulders slump, feet slap, and stomachs sag. When that happens, we begin to slow down and increase our risk of injury.

The first step to avoiding a loss of proper form is to simply be aware of what you're doing when you run. There aren't any running classes for children; no one ever teaches children to run, like they teach soccer or basketball. It's just something that we manage to naturally pick up when we're two or three years old. Nevertheless, running is a skill, and the more you become aware of how to do it the right way, the stronger you'll run.

We've already talked a bit about proper form, such as counting steps to ensure that you're taking 180 steps per minute and maintaining proper arm swing. The long run is the perfect place to work on these and other markers of proper technique. If you can learn to monitor your form in training, then you'll be able to do the same in your target race.

Listen to your foot strike. Is it suddenly louder than it was before? Have you caught your toes a few times and almost tripped? Those are signs of "floppy feet," when the muscles on the front of the lower leg are so tired that they stop raising the toes up when you lift your leg. This is called "dorsiflexion," and if you notice that you've stopped doing it properly, you can restore it if you concentrate on what you're doing.

Be aware also of your body posture. If you find yourself slouching, here's something to focus on: tightening the muscles of your core. The most important of these, for our purposes, is the transverse abdominus, which we'll talk more about later when we discuss training your core muscles. The transverse abdominus is the deepest layer of muscle in your midsection, responsible for balance and body rotation (see Fig. 4.1a on p.66). This makes it perhaps the most important core muscle involved in running. If you can hold it tight while running, you will naturally put the pelvis in a proper position for running and engage the other muscles of the core to carry their load.

The final consideration is to decide how far you ultimately need to run. The long run prepares your body for the target race distance, but the idea of a race is to challenge yourself to run as fast as possible, so simply covering the distance isn't usually the only goal. That's where *overdistance training* comes in. By exceeding the target race distance in training, you build up a reserve of endurance that will allow you to push the pace on race day.

For shorter races, such as a 5K, 10K, or even a half-marathon, this approach makes sense. But things get more complicated when the race in question is a marathon. That's because the benefits of overdistance training don't come free; there's a price to be paid by your body for very long efforts. Long training runs, even if done more slowly than your goal race pace, still put significant wear and tear on your body. At some point, the benefits to be had from an extra-long run are outweighed by the risk of injury you are exposed to by doing it. For most coaches, that point comes at runs of over 22 miles, or two and a half hours.

Some coaches, however, are willing to take that risk and recommend running longer than 22 miles when training for a marathon. I don't, so you won't find a marathon training run in this book longer than 22 miles. Remember our motto: every step necessary, but not one step more.

Alternatives

Sometimes it's not convenient or safe to go for your usual long run. Or maybe you're slammed at work and can't manage to get away for a two- or three-hour stretch during the day, even on weekends. These are the times when we need to be flexible and creative, doing the best we can to stay on course.

We talked earlier about using the treadmill, and that's certainly an option for the long run. I sympathize with all those people who complain that running on the treadmill is like watching grass grow, that it turns one of

ENGAGING THE TRANSVERSE ABDOMINUS

Before you can actively involve this muscle, you have to first get acquainted with what it feels like to flex it. Try this exercise. Stand relaxed, breathing easily. Place one palm lightly across your stomach, barely touching it. Now suck in your stomach slightly, just enough to move your stomach away from your hand. Don't tilt your pelvis or round your back to draw your stomach in; just pull your abs. Notice the slight feeling of contraction across your midsection. That's your transverse abdominus at work.

On your long run, practice pulling in your stomach the same way—just slightly, as in our exercise. It will take more concentration and focus than you might expect, so aim to keep the practice up for just a few moments at a time, and slowly build up to minutes and eventually to your entire run. If you can master this technique and apply it during your race, you'll ensure that you're running correctly. Over the course of a long race, this can make all the difference between a stumble to the finish line and a PR-setting effort.

Aim to refer back to your form checklist every 10 to 15 minutes while running. Think of it much like glancing down at the dashboard while driving—just a quick check to make sure everything is all right.

life's most enjoyable activities into a boring death march. At least when you do speed work on a treadmill, you're dividing time into small chunks, which makes it all seem to pass quicker. But that's not the case with the long run.

Unless, of course, you make the treadmill long run similar to running intervals by adapting the stepladder workout. We do this by making a change every minute or so. You can slowly increase the speed or incline of the treadmill, building up to a crescendo, and then coming back down again. You can even do multiple peaks and valleys in a workout.

Breaking up the workout this way makes it seem more manageable, much as breaking up a race into mile segments makes it seem less daunting. After all, even after running over 150 marathons, I still find it hard to imagine running 26 miles. But running a mile 26 times in a row doesn't seem all that bad.

Sometimes, however, it isn't the boredom that poses a problem; it's the scheduling. If you're finding it hard to set aside 3 hours or so during the day, consider breaking your run into two or more manageable pieces spaced out through the day. Because the body needs more than a full day to replace lost glycogen, a workout broken into segments will still train the body to burn fat as fuel as well as a single long run if you get in all of your running within 24 hours.

Are two or more shorter runs completed in one day as good as one long run, then? Not exactly. You'll hit the mark on the fuel usage, but you won't be acclimatizing the mind or body to the experience of running very long distances. After all, your target race won't be run in segments, with hours of rest and refueling available between each. Still, even if it's not ideal, a broken run is better than no long run at all.

THE TEMPO RUN
Why We Do It

Up to now we've included in our routine workouts that dance around the target race pace. We've run much faster than that pace while on the track and slower than that pace on our long runs. With the tempo run, we start closing in on the bull's-eye.

Different coaches have different definitions and ideas about the tempo run, but they all agree on this: It's a long-distance speed workout that exposes the body more directly to the rigors of actual racing. The tempo run accomplishes two things. First, it trains the body to maintain a high level of energy output over a prolonged period of time. This more closely mimics race conditions than the other workouts do. The result is adaptations made across the board by the body, including making energy usage more efficient, building up the bones and ligaments, and acclimatizing the body to a faster running cadence for a prolonged period of time.

Second, the tempo run trains the mind to stay calm and focused despite the rigors of high-intensity work. All of our running workouts should build confidence, but the tempo run, perhaps more than track workouts or the long run, shows us most directly that we are capable of holding our desired pace for mile after mile. When coaches say, "Train like you'll race and race like you've trained," this is what they're talking about.

How to Do It

The tempo run can take many forms. Some coaches recommend an out-and-back run, where the return trip is run at a faster pace than the outward-bound leg. Other coaches like a gradual build-up to a target pace, with an equally gradual descent.

The tempo run that I recommend is a steady, even workout run at a fast pace. It will last anywhere from 4 to 8 miles, depending on the length of your target race distance and where you are in your training cycle. The pace should be anywhere between your target race pace and 15 seconds per mile faster than that. For specific workout distances, refer to the training schedules in Chapter 9.

Begin your tempo workout by doing an easy 1-mile warm-up. Start at a very easy pace, and gradually speed up as you feel your breathing settling down and your muscles getting warm. Hit your pace, and hold it for the pre-determined length of your workout.

If you don't use a GPS unit to monitor your pace, aim to run on a familiar route so that you can monitor your pace with a regular chronograph watch, keying off familiar landmarks. If that's not an option, perhaps because you're running an unfamiliar route, you can once again rely on RPE. Aim to nail your tempo at around 7–8.

The tempo run is as close as you come to racing in your workouts, so it's important that you use this workout to develop good habits. Monitor your form. Are your elbows bent and hands relaxed, with your arms swinging from your shoulders and not across your upper body? Is your head held up and is your gaze on a point down the road instead of down at your feet? Are you monitoring your leg turnover and maintaining an upright posture? Are you running quietly and not with a loud slapping foot strike?

It may be difficult to think of all these things as you're running at the edge of discomfort, but that's exactly what we're aiming to become acclimated to. After all, to paraphrase the poem "If" by Rudyard Kipling, if you can keep your head when all others are losing theirs and fill the unforgiving minute with 60 seconds' worth of run, then all the world is yours and everything in it.

That's a pretty good confidence boost to bring to the starting line.

Alternatives

We've seen how the treadmill can be a viable training alternative to running on the roads for both speed work and the long run. The same holds true for the tempo run, although relying on the treadmill here requires a different kind of focus.

The difficult part of doing a tempo run on the treadmill is that holding a challenging pace for a significant period of time can be difficult enough without the boredom of staring at the same scenery mile after mile. Because it's hard to relax and become as truly distracted on a tempo run as it is on a long run, even watching TV may not be a good enough distraction. And unlike a speed workout, the hard effort can't be broken up into segments to make it more manageable.

On the other hand, one of the benefits of doing a tempo run on a tread-mill is that once you're warmed up, you can set the pace and forget it. No need to constantly hit the speed button as you would during a speed work-out. And even though this run might be difficult—and honestly, it would still be difficult outdoors on the roads or trails—at least you can be con-fident of exactly what you've accomplished, knowing the exact pace that you've run.

3

Crosstraining

CROSSTRAINING IN THE SMART MARATHON TRAINING PROGRAM is defined as any *aerobic* exercise that involves modes of training other than running. Under this definition, some modes of training that are important for us, such as core work and strength training, don't qualify as crosstraining because they don't work in the aerobic zone. We'll discuss those training modes in depth in the next chapters.

WHY CROSSTRAIN AT ALL?

The rationale for crosstraining is simple: Your heart and cardiovascular system don't care exactly what you do to get them in shape, so any exercise that causes an adaption response in these systems, whether in the gym or on the roads, will prepare you to some degree for a long-distance road race. Crosstraining enables you to get in some big cardio workouts without putting a lot of wear and tear on the body. As a result, it can help you build a big cardio base more quickly and effectively than can be accomplished by running alone.

Here's why: We know that running can be hard on the body because of the impact forces that it generates. But it's not just the pounding that's responsible for the soreness we feel after a hard workout or race. Running is also hard on the body because of the unique nature of the movement. Most contractions involve a shortening of the muscle, as when we flex our elbow and contract our biceps. But not so with running. On landing, the knee on the supporting leg is extended and the hamstring muscles there are stretched.

Although the hamstring muscles are not shortened at that point, they are nevertheless contracted. This contraction is called an eccentric, or negative, contraction. It's particularly challenging to muscle tissue because it stresses the muscle in two ways simultaneously—by compression and extension. This results in a greater microtrauma to muscle tissue than usually takes place after work is done.

In weight training, eccentric contractions are good because the added stress of the negative phase of an exercise creates a greater adaptation stimulus. For example, pushing up a barbell on a bench press is not what really works the chest muscle and causes postworkout soreness; slowly lowering the barbell down to the chest does.

In running, however, this added trauma can leave muscles more susceptible to injury. As we've discussed, we manage that risk by limiting running to three targeted workouts per week. But this alone might not be enough to create that deep reservoir of endurance that we'll need for a PR effort in a long-distance race.

That's where crosstraining comes in. Most crosstraining options avoid the impact forces involved with running and leave you less sore and tired the following day. As a result, it's possible to get in a long crosstraining workout without having to schedule a lengthy recovery period afterward. That makes it a crucial component of the training program, allowing you to get in big workouts on days that would otherwise be filled with easy, less-productive recovery runs.

OPTIONS AND CONSIDERATIONS

There are many crosstraining options available, but not all of them are of equal value to runners. In choosing between them, keep three considerations in mind:

1. **Is this option aerobic?** As we talked about earlier, one of the main adaptations that your body makes to endurance training is learning to use its fat stores as fuel. To be effective, any crosstraining mode that you choose should help you achieve this goal. That means it has to be an exercise that you can engage in for hours at a time, at a moderate intensity level (at an RPE of 6–7).

2. **Is this option low-impact or nonimpact?** Sometimes high-impact exercise gets a bad rap. When faced with repetitive impact, your body adapts, increasing bone density and strengthening the muscles related to absorbing this impact. If you don't engage in high-impact exercise, your body will be unprepared for the stress of race day. The result? A bone bruise or stress fracture.

   But remember our motto: every step necessary, but not one step more. High-impact exercise is crucial, but after the essential benefits have been gained from engaging in it, high-impact exercise raises the risk of injury during training. Running three days a week will prepare your body for the stress of racing. After that, you should aim to increase your endurance base without adding unnecessary stress to your body. This is where crosstraining comes in; it will help you achieve your race-day goals while lowering the risk of injury associated with intense high-impact training.

3. **Does this option complement your running?** Any aerobic crosstraining will help you become a better endurance athlete, but to get the most from your routine, you should choose a crosstraining mode that doesn't simply mimic the running movement, but instead works different muscle groups. The point of doing this is to strengthen the muscles that support your running. After all, your running muscles— particularly your gluteus maximus, hamstrings, and calves—are already strong from running. By focusing on strengthening your other muscles, you'll become a more balanced, injury-resistant athlete.

So what crosstraining exercise should you choose? Much of that depends on what your preferences are. Would you rather train in the great outdoors, or does the convenience of a gym appeal to you? Are you looking for a low-budget exercise that you can do anywhere, or are you intrigued by a new high-tech machine? There are plenty of options to choose from, both traditional and cutting-edge. All of them provide an added benefit of one kind or another for runners.

Four popular crosstraining modes are cycling, swimming, elliptical exercise, and stepping. All are low- or nonimpact exercises that provide excellent aerobic workouts. That makes all of these valuable training options for runners. The elliptical trainer and the stepper in particular are good substitutes for running when running isn't possible—when you're injured, for example. But apart from reducing the volume of impact, working on these machines won't add anything to your running that running itself doesn't provide. Of the four crosstraining options above, only one effectively works muscle groups that are *complementary* to running: cycling.

Perhaps you're thrilled to read that because you are already an avid fan of cycling, but if not, don't be discouraged. An old coaching aphorism is that the best exercise is one that you'll keep doing. So if you have another form of aerobic exercise that you currently enjoy, feel free to continue doing it. But my goal in this book is to make you a faster runner with the lowest risk of injury, so keep an open mind as I explain why I think cycling should be your number one crosstraining choice.

Cycling primarily works the quadriceps, a big muscle group that running doesn't effectively work. Insufficient strength in the quads can allow the knees to buckle on landing during the foot-plant phase. This is the primary cause for the up-and-down bobbing motion seen in some runners, which can lead to patella tendinitis and other knee problems. Cycling can help with that.

Cycling also works the outer hips and gluteus medius muscles, which are crucial for running. These muscles help keep the hips from swaying outward on the landing phase. When this happens, the iliotibial band—a thick strip of connective tissue on the outside of the leg—is pulled tight, which can result in knee and hip pain. Again, cycling can help with this.

Cycling also provides you a chance to take your workout outdoors, something important to many runners. Even though there are ways in which you could take your cycling workout indoors—we'll talk about these later in this chapter—cycling, for most people, represents a chance to get out for some fresh air.

For runners, this is a natural fit. You probably fell in love with running not in the gym but on the roads and trails, just like the rest of us. During our workouts and races, we have the opportunity to experience the sublime beauty of a sunrise or sunset, the changing of the seasons, or the thrill of extreme weather. Giving this up to spend time in the gym is one of the biggest hurdles some of my training clients have to overcome. But with a good bicycle, you don't have to give up your love of exploring during your workout.

Being outdoors also helps ward off the biggest problem with indoor crosstraining workouts: boredom. You *can* do a 3- or 4-hour session on an elliptical machine, but who would really *want* to? But a 3- or 4-hour bike ride is not only commonplace among cyclists; it's also considered fun. On a bike, you can cover wide stretches of territory, and with a little planning, you can map out a grand tour that includes beautiful local scenery, as well as key rest stops.

You can also more easily rope friends into joining you, which makes this a much more social form of crosstraining than the other modes. Don't have any cycling friends? It shouldn't be too difficult to find some. Most town and cities have cycling clubs. Stop by a local cycling shop and ask; staff will be happy to fill you in on all the local options.

If, despite this discussion, you still prefer supplementing your running with other forms of crosstraining, you can adjust the training schedules in Chapter 9 to suit your individual needs. For swimming, aim to spend half as much time in the pool as you would for a bicycle workout on the schedules found later in this book. For the elliptical machine and stepper, spend 75 percent as much time working out as you would if you were cycling.

CYCLING
Getting a Bicycle
Although an entry-level, quality road bike might seem relatively expensive, I guarantee you that you will soon see this as one of the best training purchases you've ever made. There are many brands, models, and types of

bikes available, made from a variety of materials and fitted with a variety of components. Don't be intimidated. A knowledgeable bike shop salesperson can guide you expertly through the process. There are also many Web sites that can explain everything you need to know about buying a bike, as well as provide reviews of any bike you're considering.

One important decision to be made is what material you prefer for the frame. Don't automatically assume that lightest—or most expensive—is best. Often the best option comes down to what kind of riding you do and what feels most comfortable.

The difference in materials generally translates into a difference in how much the bike may flex when you ride it. A more flexible bike—and we're only talking about a slight flex here, something a less experienced rider may hardly notice—will provide a bit of shock absorption on rougher roads. But there's a consequence for that bit of comfort: A more flexible frame will also bend slightly with the force of each pedal stroke, resulting in a slight loss of power as it's transferred from your muscles to the pedals and down to the road. Flexible bikes are usually made from carbon fiber, a very light but very strong material that can be very expensive.

A more rigid, or stiff, bike frame will transfer every bit of movement from your legs down to the spinning wheels, making your riding more efficient. It will also allow for a better "feel" of the road, in much the same way a pair of flip-flops allows a better feel of the ground than a pair of thick-soled hiking boots. The downside of a stiff frame, however, is that you don't necessarily want to feel the road when it's particularly rough. Also, rigid bikes tend to be heavier, although that varies with the particular material and bike. Stiff frames are often made from steel or aluminum.

Some bikes split the difference by incorporating carbon in the seat stays, which are the thin tubes running from the seat post to the back wheel. The flexibility of the carbon acts a little like shock absorbers, while the rest of the frame could be made from stiffer—and cheaper—aluminum.

Components are the other big-ticket item on your bike. This refers to the gears and shifters, which come as a set. The big difference between very cheap components and the more expensive "gruppos," as these are sometimes referred to, is that the cheap ones are machine-punched and often don't mesh as well with the bike chain, whereas the expensive ones are hand-tooled and fitted and thus will deliver a smoother, more efficient ride.

Don't make the mistake of thinking that you need to become an expert in order to buy a bike. That kind of thinking can lead to mental paralysis. Most of the time, "good enough" really does work out well. As a good rule of thumb, however, you should aim to buy all the bike you can afford. You really do get what you pay for.

Of course, that doesn't mean that you can't look for a bargain. Keep an eye open for sales at your local bike shop. Just like auto dealerships, these stores

IS A FOLDIE AN OPTION FOR YOU?

As gas prices rose across the United States in 2009 and 2010, a new urban phenomenon developed in many cities: a sudden increase in bike commuting. Among the new rigs on the roads was a breed that had until recently been mostly an oddity: the folding bicycle, or "foldie."

A foldie typically has smaller-than-usual wheels, a quickly removable seat and a movable handlebar post, and a break in the middle of the frame so that the bike can be folded in half. Foldies are designed to provide mobility for people who have little storage space in their homes, no reliable bike lockup area at work, or a desire to bring their bike with them on public transportation that won't allow a full-size bike aboard.

Foldies accomplish all of these tasks. However, a foldie can be more than a commuting tool. It can actually be a viable training option for people who need the kind of logistical flexibility such a bike provides.

Most foldies will never be the equivalent of a traditional road bike because their smaller wheels compromise handling to some degree and because most don't have the gear options of traditional road bikes, leaving a rider unable to find the right gear to climb a hill or to really hammer down a descent. Still, a foldie can be a feasible crosstraining option. Any bike that can fit easily into a car trunk, closet, or extra-large suitcase creates possibilities for getting in a workout when none would be otherwise possible.

need to move stock at the end of each season to make room for new models. That's the time to find a great deal on a new bike.

While you're looking for a new bike, don't feel that you've got to make a perfect decision. This is not a once-in-a-lifetime purchase. Most cyclists go through many bicycles; even though most will keep a bike for at least a few years, it's not unusual for cyclists to own several bikes at a time and to replace one every season. The result is a strong market for perfectly serviceable used bikes, especially online at e-auction sites or classifieds. So if you find yourself itching to upgrade to a faster bike, it won't be hard to find a buyer for your old bike. And if you don't mind riding a used bike, this is also an excellent way to upgrade to a better one yourself.

Cycling Position, Fit, and Gear

Before you head out for a killer crosstraining workout on your new wheels, we need to review a few key pre-ride basics. First, ensure that your bike seat is set at the proper height and position. I highly recommend getting a professional bike fitting if it's within your means and it's a service offered by your local bike shop. This involves detailed measurement of your body and your mechanics by a trained technician, who then makes adjustments to your bicycle to ensure an optimum fit. The result is a more efficient transfer of power from your legs to the wheels, with less stress on your hips and knees.

Imagine your pedal stroke as a clock face. When the pedal is at the 3 o'clock position, your knee should be over the ball of your foot. When the pedal is at 6 o'clock, your knee should be slightly bent. Viewed from the front, your hip, knee, and ankle should all stack up in a straight line throughout your pedal stroke.

Next, let's examine how you ride. Most people learned to ride when they were 5 years old or so and haven't given it much thought since. But just as with running, a little effort put into knowing and maintaining proper form goes a long way.

Think of your cardiovascular system and skeletal muscles as your engine and your leg and foot bones as your transmission. You don't want to generate a lot of power only to lose it though sloppy mechanics as you try to move this power to the wheels.

Your legs and especially your feet are levers that transmit power from your body to the pedals. The more flexible these levers are, the more power they will lose as you ride. Just as with your bike frame, any flexibility in your foot will translate into lost power. A rigid cycling shoe will turn your foot into a lever, transmitting much more of the power you generate directly to the pedals and giving you a mechanical advantage over a flexible shoe. Cycling shoes are well worth the investment (Fig. 3.1).

3.1

Clipless pedals also provide another mechanical advantage. Similar to ski bindings, clipless pedals allow you to lock your cycling shoes directly onto the bike (Fig. 3.2). To release, simply twist your foot laterally. If you've never used them, here's the single best piece of advice I can give you: Don't forget to unclip well before you need to stop.

Most cyclists underestimate how much time they need to get their foot free when they use clipless pedals for the first time and how quickly they lose momentum as they slow down. The result? An embarrassing topple sideways— usually at a red light, with other cyclists standing neatly around you, and motorists and pedestrians streaming by. When this happens to you—and it will—you'll hurt nothing but your ego. Remember that I told you so, take the mishap as a lesson learned, and be on your way.

3.2

So how does all this translate into actually riding faster and more powerfully? Imagine again the rotation of your pedals as a clock face. Using regular pedals, you can apply power mostly just on the 1 o'clock to 5 o'clock phase (Fig. 3.3). If you use cages—those brackets attached to the

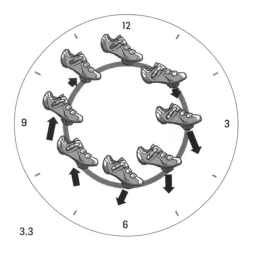

3.3

pedals into which you slip your foot—you can extend that from about 1 o'clock to 7 o'clock and maybe even a bit more if you get skilled at it. But with clipless pedals, you have the potential to apply power smoothly around the clock, which will give you a better workout and make you a better cyclist.

The key to achieving a complete pedal stroke is to focus on making it as round as possible and learning to pull back on the upstroke. Most people naturally focus only on the downstroke while pedaling because this is where most of the power is generated. But if you can learn to pull straight back and up on the pedals when each passes the 6 o'clock point on the stroke, you can be more efficient and generate more power, which will be especially helpful when riding up a hill.

Shifting Gears

Working your gears can seem more intimidating and technical than it needs to be. We're going to simplify the process into two basic rules. First, avoid crosschaining. This occurs when you choose the farthest outside chain ring in the front and the closest inside chain ring in the back, or vice versa. The result is that the chain is pushed sideways to its very limit, which puts more strain on it than it was designed to handle. This weakens the chain over time and shortens its lifespan, but in the short term this strain can also cause an annoying clicking sound because the chain will not be able to cleanly mesh with the gears.

Second, set the gear where it is comfortable. To be most efficient, avoid pushing hard in high gears; this just puts extra strain on your muscles and knees. Also remember that generally speaking, cyclists go faster by spinning more, not harder. Aim for an easy cadence of 80 to 95 pedal revolutions per minute.

Just as you can develop an accurate sense of speed while running, you can develop an inner sense of your pedaling rate, or cadence, while cycling. Of course, some clues are easy to spot. If you have to stand up out of the saddle or rock the bike laterally back and forth, you're in a gear that's too difficult. Conversely, if you can coast easily without pedaling at all or if you're wiggling in your saddle because the gear you chose is too easy, it's time to shift to a harder gear.

In general, aim to ride in the easiest gear possible, maintaining as fast a pedal cadence as you can. That's one of the secrets of the top cycling pros. It's reported that Lance Armstrong rode to his seventh Tour de France victory largely on his ability to maintain an unusually high cadence.

Also, don't be afraid to use your shifters. You should be shifting gears frequently on long rides in order to maintain a high, even cadence over changing terrain. The shifting lever on your left moves the front derailleur, which makes a major change in your effort level. The shifting lever on your right controls the rear derailleur, which fine-tunes your effort level. More often than not, except on the biggest hills, you'll be using the shifter on your right. But don't wait until you hit a hill before you practice shifting; work through all your gears one by one while riding at an easy pace.

Getting Fast by Using Cycling Drills

The main purpose of our crosstraining, as discussed, is to complement our long runs. These are not speed-building workouts; instead, they're intended to broaden our endurance base. But that doesn't mean we should completely ignore speed. Because the recovery time for crosstraining is faster than it is for running, even for the longest and most brutal workouts, we can include some speed work without fear that we'll have to schedule more rest days.

Just as with running, the way to get fast on the bike is to do form drills and practice riding faster. The best cyclists in the world aren't different from the rest of us just because they ride on bikes worth more than the car I drive (although that's certainly part of it); it's because they know how to recruit the big powerhouse muscles of their legs. The following five drills will help you start doing that, too. Perform them for 5 minutes each after a 10-minute warm-up or immediately after completing a long ride.

CYCLING DRILLS

SCRAPING THE BOTTOM OF YOUR SHOE. Practice leading the downstroke with your heels and then tip the toes down and back, as if you were scraping mud off the bottom of your shoes.

OVER THE TOP. A cardinal sin in cycling is to "toe pedal," which is to pedal with your toes pointed down more than necessary. Cycling this way engages your small calf muscles instead of your large hamstring muscles, which generally puts you at a power disadvantage. Learn to avoid this by practicing pushing your toes forward in your shoe between 10 and 2 on the pedal rotation.

JAMMERS. This is an all-out effort for 15 seconds, with an 8-minute easy-pedaling recovery, similar to running repeats on the track. Begin with 2 repetitions, then add 1 repetition each time the drill is performed, topping out at 4.

LONG SPRINTS. If jammers are like running repeats on the track, then long sprints are like tempo runs. Aim to keep a high pace for 5 to 10 minutes. Then back off, and repeat after a 10- or 15-minute rest of easier cycling.

ONE-LEGGED CYCLING. This drill helps you improve your pedal stroke by forcing you to apply power over a greater range, and also strengthens your hamstring muscles. Clip in only with your right foot, thus leaving your left foot unavailable to push the pedal once your right foot has passed below the 6 o'clock position. To keep the pedal moving, you'll have to pull on the pedals with the right foot. Once the right foot has swung up and over the 12 o'clock position, it can push again.

Do this drill for 60 seconds, then switch, and repeat 4 times. Build up until you can do 5 repeats of 2 minutes.

HIGH CADENCE. Easy spinning at a high cadence teaches proper form and builds muscle endurance. Practice cycling on a flat road on an easy gear, spinning as fast as you can without wobbling and bouncing on your saddle. Do this for 5 minutes, then resume normal cycling for 5 minutes, and then repeat.

Working the Hills

Cycling at a good cadence of 80–100 rpms builds muscle endurance (see "high cadence" cycling drill on p.58), but just as with running, you should plan to hit the hills as well. Cycling on varied terrain—flat straightaways, rolling hills, big climbs—provides a range of training stimuli for your body and will deliver better overall fitness than doing the same routine over and over again. For that reason, you also want to be sure to include those hills on your routes at least once per week. Working the hills once a week, especially the big climbs, builds both power and speed by triggering adaptations in your fast-twitch muscle fibers.

Just as with running hills, however, you don't need to plan your hill rides with precise exactitude. Some training plans recommend specific grades and distances. I don't know anyone who measures their routes this way, and you don't need to do that either. Instead, try to find several hilly areas where you can ride.

One route that you should map out would contain a few big climbs or one big climb that you could repeat 3–6 times. What constitutes a big climb? Use former Supreme Court Justice Potter Stewart's definition of pornography: You'll know it when you see it. If midway through the hill you're asking yourself if it's worth it, and by the top of the hill your legs feel wobbly and you're gasping for air, it's a big climb.

A second option should be a ride that contains "rollers," which are a series of easy hills, situated one after the other.

Safety

Several years ago I woke up to find myself sitting in the street next to my bicycle, disoriented and bleeding from cuts on my hands and face. To this day I don't know exactly what happened, but my guess is that I was clipped from behind by a car and sent flying. The impact cracked my helmet nearly in half.

The moral of the story is that an accident can happen in the blink of an eye and as a cyclist you're in a vulnerable position. Increase the odds of making it home safe and sound after every ride by showing good common sense while cycling. To that end, we're going to review the following few basic safety rules:

1. **Ride defensively.** Stay alongside traffic, and obey all signs and signals.
2. **Wear bright clothing.** And if you must ride at night, remember to have a white light in the front of your bike so that you can see cars and a red light on the back of your bike so that they can see you.
3. **Never ride without a helmet.** Every cyclist I know has gotten into one or more crashes, resulting in injuries ranging from simple road rash to complicated fractures requiring multiple surgeries. Wearing a helmet is one thing you can do to increase the chances that you'll survive to ride another day.
4. **Always carry identification.** Be sure to also have emergency contact information, as well as any pertinent medical information that would be helpful to a first responder.

If you do get into an accident, be sure to carefully assess your body for possible injuries and your bike for damage. Sometimes the effects of an accident—especially regarding injuries—are not apparent at first. If another person is involved, whether a pedestrian, cyclist, or driver, take all relevant information. Also be sure to seek medical attention as soon as possible, especially if you suspect an injury.

Taking Cycling Indoors

We've talked about the joys of cycling outdoors, but this is not always an option. A cycling friend once spelled this out for me clearly: When the temperatures drop, there comes a point at which your efforts to warm up by going faster create a windchill that you can never overcome. Despite best efforts and the protections of whatever heavy-weather gear you've bought, you only seem to get colder and colder as the workout progresses. He put this limit at somewhere around 35°F.

Low temperatures aren't the only reason that outdoor cycling can become difficult or impossible. Heavy rain, sleet, snow, or fog can make cycling dangerous. If you're ever in doubt about whether you should head out the door for a workout, the answer is that you probably shouldn't. Remember that no single workout will make you a better athlete and no single workout is worth risking serious injury. Be prepared for those difficult days

---

CHOOSING A HELMET

Much of the difference between the highest-priced helmets and the lower-end models is the effort made by the manufacturer to make the helmet as light as possible, providing maximum ventilation while still providing maximum protection. That's all fine and good, but you don't need to shell out $200 or more to protect your crown. Check out helmet reviews online to get an idea of your options, and then investigate a variety in your neighborhood shop. Check the fit by strapping the helmet on and then shaking your head side to side and up and down. A good fit will allow very little movement of the helmet while still feeling comfortable.

Once you have a model in mind, check to see that it's been certified as complying with safety standards set by the U.S. Consumer Product Safety Commission. Helmets are often certified by reputable, independent testing organizations, such as the American National Standards Institute.

Once you've purchased your helmet, customize it by cutting away the excess strap and burning the end with a match to seal it.

---

by having a plan to take your crosstraining workout indoors. There are several options.

1. **Hit the gym.** If you belong to a fitness center—and I recommend that you do so that you can do all of the exercises that you'll see in Chapters 4 and 5—the easiest thing to do is to join a spinning class or spend time on a stationary bike (Fig. 3.4).

2. **Buy an indoor trainer.** An indoor stationary trainer converts your bicycle into a stationary workout station. It's a small piece of equipment that attaches to the rear of your bicycle (Fig. 3.5). When set up, your rear wheel will engage a roller on the trainer, which provides adjustable resistance to your spinning. This is a space-efficient, inexpensive option that will give you maximum flexibility because you can jump on your bike at any hour without even leaving your living space. Set the trainer up in front of your TV and settle in for a long session.

3. **Get rolling.** Indoor cycling offers great convenience, but the downside of indoor training is not just the lack of changing scenery but also the lack of practice balancing your bicycle. That extra bit of work—hardly noticeable most of the time—helps strengthen the stabilizing muscles of your core in a way that a stationary bike doesn't.

Rollers change all that. This apparatus has been described as a cross between an indoor treadmill and a logrolling contest for your bicycle (Fig. 3.6). Consisting of three rollers contained within a frame, it requires you to balance your bike as you pedal, resulting in a workout that feels much more like cycling on the open road. Rollers are not as commonly used as stationary trainers, but among the die-hards who master the roller, it's considered the best way to train indoors.

DETERMINING THE BEST INDOOR TRAINING OPTION FOR YOU

Having choices means that you'll have to make a decision about which is the right indoor training option for you. Given that all of these options are effective, you can't go wrong, but you'll still have to pick one. Let me give you the pros and cons of each, as well as my personal recommendation.

STATIONARY BIKE/SPIN BIKE IN A GYM.
One pro is that these machines are very stable, which allows you to enjoy the distraction of reading a magazine or watching TV while working out. Because you'll likely be going to a gym to use one, another pro is that you'll be able to access high-end machines easily.

The main con is that because you'll be so stable on the machine, you won't be engaging your core muscles.

3.4

INDOOR TRAINER. This piece of equipment differs from a stationary bike in that it incorporates your regular bike into an indoor training apparatus. All you need to do is retrieve your trainer from the closet, bolt your bike in place, put your front tire in the stabilizing block, and get on for a ride. You

3.5

can set up in front of your TV and settle in for a nice workout. The main pro is that you can easily use this equipment in your own home. The main con, however, is that to some extent the quality of your workout will be dictated by the quality of your bike.

ROLLERS. The main pro here is that because your bike will be riding free on this machine, you'll be actively engaging your core as you work out and struggle to keep your balance.

As with the indoor trainer, however, the major con is that you'll need your own bike. The learning curve on this one is pretty steep, too; expect to have some trouble and some bruises before you master it. You'll need to focus while on the rollers, so avoid outside distractions—no reading during these workouts!

3.6

Bottom line: I recommend joining a gym. You'll have access to high-level equipment, and even if you don't engage the core much on the stationary bike or spinner, you'll cover that base in your other workouts.

4

Building a Runner's Body, Part 1

FUNCTIONAL EXERCISES AND CORE STRENGTH PROGRAM

BY NOW YOU KNOW THAT THE CENTRAL PHILOSOPHY of this book is that in order to become the best runner you can be, you need to do more than just run. In the preceding chapters, we talked about the essential running workouts that make up the aerobic portion of this program. We're now going to talk about anaerobic exercises that you need to do to support your running and make you a healthier, more complete athlete.

In this chapter, you'll find a large number of exercises divided into two main groups: running-specific, or functional, exercises and core exercises. The functional exercises will strengthen the muscles that are directly involved in running, often in the same way that they are used in running. Core work strengthens the powerful muscles of the midsection, which help stabilize the body during *all* movement, not just running. Think of core work as building a solid, general foundation that suits many purposes, whereas running-specific exercises build a specialized tower that rises above it.

To some extent, many of the exercises here overlap, as some traditional core exercises may be especially useful to runners and many running-specific exercises engage the core. No need to split hairs on names; taken together, these exercises will make you a better runner.

Also, don't feel overwhelmed by the number of exercises; you won't have to do all of them in every workout. In fact, your strength workouts will be quick and short, as you pick from the options that we'll be reviewing here. In this way, no two workouts have to be the same back-to-back, which will help keep both you and your body from getting bored. We'll review exactly how this will work at the end of this chapter.

But for now, we're going to impose order on these exercises by squeezing them into different categories. After reviewing the key muscles groups, we'll discuss the running-specific exercises, including floor exercises, standing exercises, balancing and lunging, and jumps—or plyometrics, as these are sometimes called. Following these exercises, we'll review the more general core work that will be part of your routine.

As you review the exercises listed in the following pages, you'll notice that for some there are two or more options presented: a basic method and one or more advanced versions, marked with a [+]. When trying an exercise for the first time or returning to an exercise after a significant layoff, begin with the basic version until your strength and balance improve. Once you feel comfortable and ready to take on more of a challenge, add some of the different advanced versions into your workout.

When you've mastered all of the advanced exercises, you'll have the option of mixing and matching the core strength exercises. The possible combinations are nearly endless.

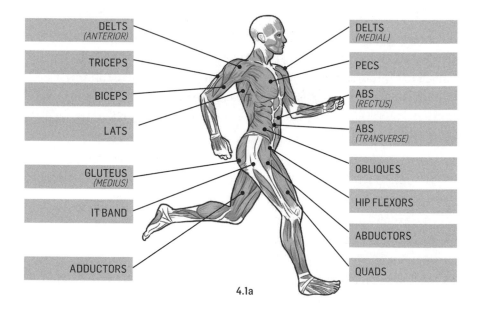

DELTS (ANTERIOR)
TRICEPS
BICEPS
LATS
GLUTEUS (MEDIUS)
IT BAND
ADDUCTORS

DELTS (MEDIAL)
PECS
ABS (RECTUS)
ABS (TRANSVERSE)
OBLIQUES
HIP FLEXORS
ABDUCTORS
QUADS

4.1a

TARGET MUSCLE GROUPS

Before we get into our routine, let's identify some of the muscle groups that we'll be targeting (Figs. 4.1a and 4.1b).

Abs (rectus). Commonly known as the six-pack muscles, these abdominal muscles are found on the front of your body. They are responsible for shortening the torso in spinal flexion, as when you curl up in a ball.

Abs (transverse). This is the deepest layer of abdominal muscle. It stabilizes your spine and pelvis and provides support for your vertebrae during intense exercise, such as running.

Adductors and abductors. These are the muscles of your inner and outer leg, respectively, which move your leg side to side. An easy way to remember which one is which is to recall that *add*uctors *add* your legs together, which leaves the abductors to spread them apart. These muscles help stabilize and power the front-and-back motion of your legs during running.

Calves. The muscles on the back of the lower leg that power the lifting of the heel during running.

Delts. This group is made up of three major muscles: the anterior deltoid in front, the medial deltoid in the middle, and the posterior deltoid in the

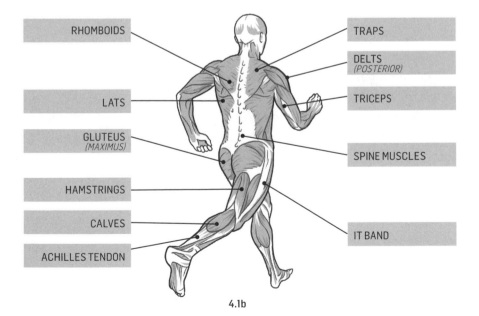

RHOMBOIDS

TRAPS

DELTS
(POSTERIOR)

LATS

TRICEPS

GLUTEUS
(MAXIMUS)

SPINE MUSCLES

HAMSTRINGS

CALVES

ACHILLES TENDON

IT BAND

4.1b

rear. Together, these muscles facilitate movement of the arms in almost all directions.

Gluteus maximus. This is one muscle group that most people can easily identify; it's the big muscle group we call our backside. Its chief function is to forcefully extend the hip, pulling the leg back. This muscle group is the big engine behind running.

Gluteus medius. This is the lesser-known glute muscle. While standing, put one hand on your side and find the point of your hip. Now slide your hand just behind it. That's your gluteus medius. It's responsible for maintaining lateral hip position, especially when you're off balance.

Hamstrings. These are three muscles on the back of the upper leg that together power knee flexion, as during the push-off phase of running.

Hip flexors. These are the muscles located in the front of the body near the crease of the hip and include the psoas muscle. Together, these muscles pull your legs forward in hip flexion during running.

IT band. A thick band of connective tissue that runs along the outer leg from the hip to the knee and lower leg.

Lats. These are the big muscles of the upper back. They're used to power almost all pulling motions.

Obliques Popularly called the love handles, these muscles facilitate lateral movement and twisting.

Pecs. These are the chest muscles, which power most of your pushing movements.

Quads. These are four muscles on the front of the upper leg that power knee extensions. They also help hold the kneecap in proper position during running.

Rhomboids. These muscles line the spine between your shoulder blades. They help pull your shoulder blades together, as when you pull your arms back behind you.

Spine muscles. These are the muscles of the lumbar region of your lower back. They help keep your body erect and absorb impact stress.

Traps. A large triangular muscle that straddles the spine from the base of the neck to the lower back, this muscle group helps power and stabilize most movements of the upper back.

SETTING UP THE HOME GYM: EQUIPMENT

Even though I recommend joining a fitness center in order to access treadmills, steppers, stationary bikes, cables, dumbbells, and machines, it isn't absolutely required. You could easily get in a great workout at home using just these few pieces of equipment, which are relatively inexpensive and easy to store.

BOSU. Named for the acronym for "both sides up," this apparatus looks like a half dome, with a hard, flat side, and a soft, inflated round side. You flip the BOSU on either side and stand on it to work on balance and stability.

STABILITY BALL. This large inflated ball comes in a variety of sizes and varies in quality. Some are loaded with sand to increase resistance during lifting. Any of them will be sufficient.

MEDICINE BALL. This weighted, rubberized ball is available in most sporting goods stores. It comes in a variety of weights; aim to get one that weighs 8–12 pounds.

FUNCTIONAL EXERCISES

You probably don't spend a lot of time as a runner thinking about your hips. You should; they're a big problem area for many runners. Weakness and lack of flexibility in this area can compromise your running mechanics, putting stress on your iliotibial band and knees and thereby leading to pain and injury. Most of the exercises in this section address that weakness directly.

No special equipment is needed for these other than a yoga mat or other soft surface to lie down on. At the end of this chapter, you'll find more details on incorporating these exercises into your program, but here are a few key points about these exercises:

- The order of these exercises isn't important.
- You can choose to do them in a group one after the other, or you can break them apart and do them between other exercises in your workout.
- In total, these exercises should not take more than 10 minutes to perform.
- These exercises should be a regular part of your routine.

FLOOR EXERCISES

All of these exercises are to be performed a minimum of once a week, along with whatever core exercises you choose for that workout, and they can be performed two to three times per week for better results. You'll do most of these on the ground. If you don't own a good cushioned mat, be kind to your knees and tailbone and buy one.

For those exercises in which you start on all fours, you can make the exercise more challenging by extending the arm opposite the leg you're working. This will leave you balancing on one knee and the opposite arm, which will engage your abdominals as you struggle to stay balanced.

MUSCLE TARGET
Gluteus

CLAM Lie on your left side, with legs together and knees bent (4.2a). Keeping your feet touching, raise your right knee, spreading your legs apart (4.2b). Start with 10 reps; then flip over and do the other side. Add 2 reps to each side each week until you get to 20 reps.

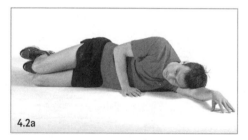

4.2a

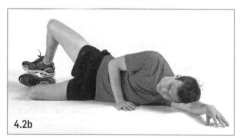

4.2b

FUNCTIONAL

SIDE LEG RAISE Lie on your left side with legs straight, one atop the other (4.3a). Raise your right leg while pointing toes outward (4.3b). Halfway through the set, turn your foot so that toes are pointing upward and continue. Start with 10 reps, and then flip over and do the other side. Add 2 reps to each side each week until you get to 20 reps.

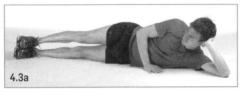

[+] ADVANCED To make this exercise more challenging and to engage your obliques and transverse abdominus, perform this exercise from a side plank position, with your body elevated and held rigid in a straight line, resting on your left elbow, with legs stacked on top of each other (4.4a and b).

FUNCTIONAL

MUSCLE TARGET

Hip flexors

Gluteus

DONKEY KICK Start on all fours (4.5a). Kick your right leg high behind you, keeping your knee bent (4.5b); then repeat with your left leg. Start with 10 reps on one side, and then do the other side. Add 2 reps to each side each week until you get to 20 reps. This exercise extends your hips, which improves their range of motion.

4.5a

4.5b

MUSCLE TARGET

Hip flexors

DONKEY WHIP Start on all fours. Swing your right leg out to the side, keeping it as straight as possible (4.6a). Sweep wide, but try to keep your hips stable as you do so. Don't twist your body in order to move your leg farther because this will work your obliques instead of your hips. Return your leg to the starting position, and continue across your midline as far as you comfortably can (4.6b). Start with 10 reps, and then do your left leg. Add 2 reps to each side each week until you get to 20 reps.

4.6a

4.6b

FIRE HYDRANT Start on all fours (4.7a). Swing your left leg out and up, keeping your knee bent (4.7b), like a puppy relieving itself by a fire hydrant (hence, the name of the exercise), and then return to the starting position. Avoid rotating your body; focus on moving only your leg. Start with 10 reps; then do your right leg. Add 2 reps to each side each week until you get to 20 reps.

MUSCLE TARGET
Gluteus
Abductors

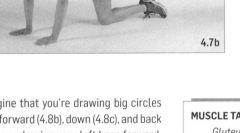

4.7a 4.7b

PRONE HURDLE Start on all fours. Imagine that you're drawing big circles with your left knee by swinging it out (4.8a), forward (4.8b), down (4.8c), and back (4.8d). After 10 repetitions, reverse direction and swing your left knee forward, up, back, and down. Repeat with your right leg. This exercise helps increase the range of motion of your hip joint.

MUSCLE TARGET
Gluteus

4.8a 4.8b
4.8c 4.8d

FUNCTIONAL

MUSCLE TARGET
Gluteus

Abs

[+] **ADVANCED** To make this exercise more difficult, hold your right hand straight in front of you as you swing your left leg (4.9a, b, and c) and then your left arm straight in front of you as you swing your right leg. This creates lateral instability, which in turn forces your abdominals to tighten.

4.9a

4.9b

4.9c

FUNCTIONAL

STANDING EXERCISES

Because these are low-impact exercises that increase blood flow and range of motion, they make an ideal warm-up before every cardio workout. Do these exercises a minimum of twice per week.

Start by bracing yourself by placing a hand against a wall or chair, but as you get familiar with these movements, rely instead on your balance to keep you steady. (We'll talk about the importance of balance for runners in the next section.)

STANDING HURDLE These are just like the Prone Hurdle reviewed previously, but performed standing. Swing your left leg in forward and backward circles 10 times (4.10a, b, and c), and then repeat with your right leg. Just as with the Prone Hurdle, this exercise helps increase the range of motion of your hip joint.

> **MUSCLE TARGET**
> *Gluteus*

4.10a

4.10b

4.10c

FUNCTIONAL

LATERAL LEG SWING   Swing your left leg past your midline (4.11a) and then out to your side as far as you can, like a big pendulum (4.11b). Aim to keep the rest of your body as still as possible. Then repeat with your right leg. Start with 10 repetitions on each side, and add 2 reps each week until you reach 20 reps. This exercise also helps increase the range of motion of your hip joint.

> **MUSCLE TARGET**
> *Gluteus*

4.11a   4.11b

FRONT LEG SWING   Swing your left leg forward and backward as far as you can, keeping the rest of your body as still as possible (4.12a and b). Then repeat with your right leg. Start with 10 repetitions on each side, and add 2 reps each week until you reach 20 reps.

> **MUSCLE TARGET**
> *Hip flexors*
> *Abs*

4.12a   4.12b

BALANCING AND LUNGING

Try this: Stand on one foot. Not so tough, right? Now close your eyes and count to 10. If you made it all 10 seconds before touching down, you're one of the few.

This simple test highlights the importance and effectiveness of your *proprioreceptors*, the muscle-nerve connections that create an awareness of our bodies in space. When you put your body in an awkward position, these proprioreceptors make tiny adjustments to help the body maintain balance. This is what keeps you from falling flat on your face when you unexpectedly step on a crack in the sidewalk or a root on a trail.

For runners, a strong network of proprioreceptors is especially important. The entire running motion is spent either in the air or balanced on one foot. Even under the best terrain and weather conditions, this presents a formidable challenge to your body.

Balance exercises help prepare your body for this motion and help reduce the risk of a sprain, strain, or other injury. But the benefits of doing balance work go beyond your running goals. As you age, your ability to balance can decrease dramatically. This not only compromises your quality of life but also increases your chances of experiencing a debilitating fall. By getting in the habit of doing balance work, you can decrease your chances of encountering these problems later in life. Do these exercises at least twice per week.

FUNCTIONAL

MUSCLE TARGET

Gluteus

Spine

ONE-LEGGED DEADLIFT Keeping your left leg planted on the ground and your hands at your sides (4.13a), tip over until you form a perfect T, with your right leg perfectly straight behind you and your torso leaning forward parallel to the ground (4.13b). Hold for 2 seconds, and then return to an upright position. Repeat. Then stand on your right leg and tip over, raising your left leg straight behind you. Make this exercise more challenging by refraining from touching down with your moving leg between repetitions. Start with 10 repetitions on each side, and add 2 reps each week until you reach 20 reps.

Be sure to keep the toes on your uplifted foot pointing downward. If you rotate your leg, you'll also be rotating your hips, which will shift your center of gravity and relieve the outward pressure on your hip. In other words, you won't be working your gluteus medius, which is why we're doing this in the first place.

4.13a

4.13b

MUSCLE TARGET

Gluteus

Spine

Abs

[+] ADVANCED To further challenge your balance and core strength, rotate your body as you do in the deadlift exercise above, reaching across your body with the arm opposite your planted leg. Now imagine that you've dropped your wallet and you're bending over to pick it up (4.14a and b). You don't need to actually touch the floor, however, and be sure to keep your back straight as you bend over. As you reach down with one arm, raise your other arm up toward the sky. Start with 10 repetitions on each side, and add 2 reps each week until you reach 20 reps.

4.14a   4.14b

LUNGE This exercise is the workhorse of leg exercises. Step forward with your right leg, and drop your body down until your left knee almost touches the floor (4.15a and b). Return to your starting position, and then step out with your left leg and repeat. Make sure that your front knee doesn't go past your toes, as that would put too much unnecessary pressure on your knees. Start with 10 repetitions on each side, and add 2 reps each week until you reach 20 reps.

If you find this exercise too difficult, concentrate on bending your back knee to drop down, rather than just bending your front knee. On the return, avoid using your upper body to generate momentum; use your legs and hips instead.

MUSCLE TARGET
Quads
Gluteus
Abductors
Adductors

4.15a   4.15b

FUNCTIONAL

MUSCLE TARGET

Quads

Gluteus

Abductors

Adductors

WALKING LUNGE As in a regular lunge, this exercise involves stepping forward and sinking down. However, instead of returning to your starting point, you continue forward, alternating legs (refer to 4.15 for proper form). Come to a full stop between lunges so that you don't build momentum, which would make the movement less precise and easier on your legs. Although this exercise works the same muscles as a standing lunge, this version puts more emphasis on the stabilizing muscles of your hips and also improves your balance.

MUSCLE TARGET

Gluteus

Hamstrings

Hip flexors

Abs

[+] ADVANCED Make this exercise more challenging by rotating your upper body over your front leg when you are in the dropped position (4.16a and b). This will destabilize your body even more and involve your core more deeply in the movement. Stretch your arms in front of you, and swing them to the side. Follow them with your eyes to ensure that you are turning your entire upper body. For an even more advanced version, hold a light dumbbell or medicine ball; 5–10 pounds would be plenty. Start with 10 lunges on each side (20 steps in all), and add 2 reps each week until you reach 20.

4.16a

4.16b

FUNCTIONAL

SIDE LUNGE With feet close together (4.17a), step out to your left side and sink down (4.17b); then return to your starting position, step to your right side, and repeat. Make sure your feet are pointing forward throughout the exercise and that your static leg is straight as you squat down on the opposite leg. Start with 10 repetitions alternating from left to right, and add 2 reps each week until you reach 20 reps.

MUSCLE TARGET
Quads
Hamstrings
Abductors
Adductors
Abs
Gluteus

WIDE SQUAT Stand with your feet spread as far apart as possible, with your arms outstretched for balance or crossed over your chest (4.18a). Squat down, keeping your backside out and your pelvis tilted, your back arched, and your chest forward (4.18b). Do not let your knees extend farther than the tips of your toes; that would indicate that you are bending the knees at less than a 90-degree angle, which puts too much strain on the knees' supporting tendons and ligaments. Start with 10 repetitions, and add 2 reps each week until you reach 20 reps.

MUSCLE TARGET
Quads
Gluteus
Adductors

FUNCTIONAL

MUSCLE TARGET

Gluteus

Quads

Abductors

NARROW SQUAT   The opposite of a wide squat, this exercise is done with the feet as close together as possible (4.19a and b). If you find that your heel lifts off the ground, don't be alarmed; you could always place a low board under your heels to provide some support. Start with 10 repetitions, and add 2 reps each week until you reach 20 reps.

4.19a

4.19b

FUNCTIONAL

JUMPS

These exercises are designed to build speed into your running by working the fast-twitch muscle fibers in your legs and hips, which are responsible for short, explosive movements. Perform each exercise quickly while still paying close attention to form. As with all of our exercises, working correctly is paramount.

Because they are higher impact than the other exercises we've reviewed, you'll need a bit more recovery time afterward. As you'll see when you review the complete program in Chapter 9, you need to do these only once per week with your functional exercises.

STEP-UPS Take a sprinter's position, with your left leg and right arm forward, both elbows bent, squatting slightly (4.20a). Swing your left arm forward and your right knee up, as if trying to jump up in the air (4.20b). Your left forefoot should stay planted on the ground, but your momentum should bring you up onto your toes. To be an explosive movement, you need to get that left heel in the air. Do 10 repetitions on your right side; then switch to your left and do 10 repetitions there. Add 2 repetitions to this exercise each week until you reach 20.

MUSCLE TARGET
Hip flexors

4.20a   4.20b

FUNCTIONAL

JUMP AND REACH With feet shoulder-width apart, squat down and try to touch the ground (4.21a), making sure that your knees don't go lower than a 90-degree angle. (As mentioned in the lunge, deep knee bends put too much stress on the knees.) Now spring up quickly and reach for the sky, jumping as high as you can (4.21b). On landing, squat down to reload, and repeat. Start with 10 repetitions, and add 2 each week until you reach 20.

4.21a

4.21b

BOX JUMP Find a safe platform approximately 1 foot high; a step riser or bench would work. Stand in front of it with feet shoulder-width apart (4.22a), and then jump up onto the platform (4.22b). Be sure to jump from both feet evenly so that both feet land on the platform simultaneously. Start with 10 repetitions, and add 2 each week until you reach 20.

4.22a

4.22b

CORE STRENGTH PROGRAM

Think of your body as a powerful platform supporting two collars—the shoulder and hip apparatus—with attached appendages to perform necessary work. These appendages—the arms and legs—move around, but they are only able to work effectively if they're grounded by a solid base.

This base is called the core. The core is defined as all the muscle groups located between your midthigh and the bottom of your ribcage, both in the front and the back. These include all the muscles of the abdominal area, as well as the hips, backside, lower back, and inner and outer leg.

"Work the core" has become the mantra of fitness classes coast to coast, but few people do it correctly and successfully. Runners in particular often either fail to include core work in their program, do too little of it, or don't include the specific exercises that would benefit them the most as runners. We're going to fix that.

To work the core effectively, you need to do more than crunches or sit-ups. In fact, traditional crunches, although a fine exercise, are far from the most effective core exercise for runners. Crunches involve spinal flexion, shortening the body as we curl our backs to bring our shoulders closer to our knees. What part of the running motion even remotely involves this kind of movement? Maybe just getting out of bed to shut off the alarm clock.

Together, the core muscles balance your body as you move and power it through the twists and turns that are a crucial part of almost every sport. Weakness in any of the core muscles not only compromises your running motion but also sets you up for injury and overall ill health.

When all the muscles of your core are strong, your body can move correctly, with all the muscle groups carrying an appropriate load. This results in potential for quicker, more powerful movements.

When core muscles are weak, however, movements are compromised, and injury can result. Chiropractor Dr. Kevin Maggs, an Ironman® triathlete and marathoner himself, reports that among athletes who come to him with running injuries, 90 percent can trace their problems to insufficient core strength.

For example, many runners suffer from tightness in the iliotibial band, a thick strip of connective tissue that attaches to the outer point of the hip (the ilium) and runs along the outside of the leg, finally connecting to the knee and the lower leg (the tibia). Tightness in this area causes the IT band to rub along the outside of the knee as it passes that area, resulting in irritation and pain. Massaging and stretching the IT band may help, but often the tightness returns. The key question is, why is the IT band tight in the first place?

Here's one possible reason: When you run, much of your time is spent balancing on one leg. You land on one leg, push off, and then land on the other leg and push off, and so on. When you're on one leg, your body is out of balance. As we've already discussed, you generate outward pressure on the hip of your support leg. If your gluteus medius isn't strong enough to resist this pressure, your hip will fall outward, causing tugging on the IT band. *That's* what leads to tightness and pain in the IT band.

This condition is easy to spot. In your next race, look at the waistband or shirt hem of the runners in front of you. You will likely notice some of them swaying wildly from side to side, like a boat in a storm, as each hip rises and falls. Now try to spot runners who lack this motion. Their waistband or shirt hem remains flat and still because their gluteus medius is holding their hips in place.

The solution is obvious: Strengthen the gluteus medius, and enable it to push back against the outward pressure created by running. Strengthening this muscle group would help resolve IT band issues and prevent their recurrence.

Not all runners have the same core weaknesses and issues, of course, which is why not all runners get the same injuries. But even though getting a particular injury can reveal core strength problems, it would be better to avoid the injury in the first place. This is why we'll work not just the gluteus medius but also all the core muscles.

Core work—indeed, most of the work in this program—differs from traditional strength training because it works the movement more than it works the muscle. That means the goal of these exercises isn't necessarily to make any body part look better but instead to make the body as a whole perform better. This focus makes the approach we take in this book a most appropriate form of training for endurance athletes because most runners don't really care how big their quadriceps or biceps are, for example, but they do care about how fast they can run.

As with the running-specific exercises reviewed earlier in this chapter, the order of these exercises and whether they are performed in a block or mixed in among other exercises are less important than the fact that they get done. For simplicity's sake, we'll divide them into three sections: upright or on a bench, on a mat, and on a stability ball.

Plan on doing at least some core work almost every day. You don't have to do the whole routine every time; target a few exercises each day, and plan to get through the entire regimen by week's end.

UPRIGHT OR ON A BENCH

CAPTAIN'S CHAIR LEG LIFT If you go to a gym, look for the station that allows you to rest on your elbows, with your legs hanging down free (4.23a). That's called a captain's chair. Climb aboard and raise your knees as high as you can, curling into a ball (4.23b). To make this more difficult, keep knees locked and legs straight. (To do this exercise at home, see Knee Crunch on p.89.) Start with 10 repetitions, and add 2 each week until you reach 20.

MUSCLE TARGET
Abs
Hip flexors
Hamstrings

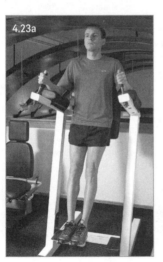

4.23a
4.23b

CORE

<table>
<tr><td>

MUSCLE TARGET

Abductors

Adductors

</td></tr>
</table>

SCISSORS Sit on a mat on the floor or an exercise bench. Place your hands on the floor or the bench to hold yourself steady, and hold your legs out straight in front of you (4.24a). Now spread your legs wide and then swing them together, letting your right leg cross over your left (4.24b). Repeat, letting your left leg cross over on this pass. Continue alternating the crossovers throughout the set. Start with 10 repetitions, and add 2 each week until you reach 20. If you would like to make this exercise more challenging, let go of the bench or floor and perform the exercise while balancing on your tailbone.

4.24a   4.24b

<table>
<tr><td>

MUSCLE TARGET

Abs

Lower back

Hip flexors

</td></tr>
</table>

V SIT-UP Balance on your tailbone, holding your legs unsupported in the air in front of you, knees locked out (4.25a). Fold your body as much as possible, raising both your legs and torso upward, like a pair of scissors closing (4.25b). Lay back and repeat. Start with 10 repetitions, and add 2 each week until you reach 20. To increase the intensity of this exercise, rotate your torso first to the right and then to the left as you rise up.

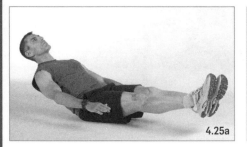

4.25a   4.25b

KNEE CRUNCH Balance on your tailbone with legs extended (4.26a), bring both knees toward your chest (4.26b), and then straighten them out again. Start with 10 repetitions, and add 2 each week until you reach 20.

MUSCLE TARGET
Abs

Hip flexors

ON A MAT

CRUNCH Lie on your back with knees bent (4.27a). Slowly roll your upper body up until your shoulder blades are off the floor (4.27b). You can cradle your head with your hands for support, but don't pull on your head or you'll risk straining your neck. Hold feet in the air during the entire exercise to increase its intensity. Start with 20 reps, and add 5 repetitions per week until you reach 50.

MUSCLE TARGET
Abs

CORE

MUSCLE TARGET
Abs

LEG RAISE Lie on your back on top of your hands (4.28a). Keeping your knees locked straight, raise your legs to a vertical position (4.28b). As you get stronger, put your hands on your stomach and keep your elbows off the floor, which forces your core to work harder to keep from getting pulled all over the floor. Start with 10 reps, and add 2 per week until you reach 20.

4.28a

4.28b

MUSCLE TARGET
Abs
Spine

[+] ADVANCED Other challenging variations include squeezing a stability ball between your ankles, which engages your adductors, or doing a high leg raise, in which you keep your hands on the floor and lift your hips up in the air once your legs are vertical (4.29a and b).

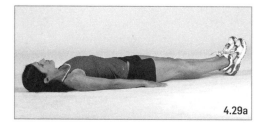
4.29a

4.29b

CORE

CROSSOVER CRUNCH Lie back and put your right foot on your left knee (4.30a). Contract your rectus abdominus, and lift your left shoulder up while twisting across toward your right, keeping your right elbow on the ground (4.30b). Do 20 reps; then repeat on the other side. Quickly work your way up to 30 repetitions by adding 5 each week.

MUSCLE TARGET
Abs

[**+**] **ADVANCED** For a more advanced version, straighten your right leg (4.31a) and raise it up and down as you twist (4.31b). Aim to touch your left hand to your right knee (although you don't actually have to touch them; that's just an image to guide your motion).

MUSCLE TARGET
Abs

CORE

MUSCLE TARGET
Lower back

Gluteus

SUPERMAN From a prone position on the mat, with arms outstretched, arch your upper body and your legs simultaneously (4.32a). Aim to keep your legs straight and to raise them from your hips (4.32b). Start with 20 reps, and work your way up to 50 by adding 5 each week.

4.32a

4.32b

MUSCLE TARGET
Obliques

WINDSHIELD WIPER Lie face up, holding your legs together straight up in the air. Keeping your hips as flat on the ground as possible, let both legs fall to one side (4.33a). Get them down as close to the mat as you can, perpendicular to your body, and then swing your legs up and over to the other side (4.33b). Start with 10 reps, and work your way up to 20 by adding 2 each week.

4.33a

4.33b

SIDE CRUNCH Lie on your side, with legs straight, one atop the other (4.34a). Raise up both legs together as you simultaneously raise up your torso (4.34b). Avoid jerking the upper body; aim to pull from your sides. Start with 20 reps; then repeat on the other side. Work your way up to 50 by adding 5 each week.

MUSCLE TARGET
Obliques

SIDE HIP RAISE Balance on your side, resting on your elbow and feet, with legs straight and body held rigid in the air (4.35a). Let your hips sink toward the floor (4.35b), then raise them back up, and repeat. Start with 20 reps; then repeat on the other side. Work your way up to 30 by adding 2 reps each week.

MUSCLE TARGET
Obliques
Gluteus

CORE

MUSCLE TARGET
Abs

Hip flexors

ROLL-UP Lie with knees slightly bent, heels on the floor (4.36a). Raise your upper body to a sitting position (4.36b); then slowly roll back down again on a 2-count. The trick is to keep your heels touching the floor the entire time. Start with 10 repetitions, and add 2 reps each week until you get to 30 reps. To make it more challenging, hold your body just off the ground when you lie back. By not touching the ground between repetitions, you'll maintain pressure on your abs throughout the entire movement.

4.36a

4.36b

MUSCLE TARGET
Gluteus

Spine

SUPINE PLANK Lie face up (4.37a). Resting on your elbows and heels, raise your body up in the air, holding it rigid (4.37b). To make this exercise more difficult, raise a leg as high in the air as possible, which engages your hip flexors. Start with 5 repetitions on each leg, and add 1 each week until you get to 10.

4.37a

4.37b

CIRCLES Lie face up, arms on the ground out to your sides. Raise up your legs, and hold them together (4.38a). Now rotate legs clockwise, drawing big circles with your feet (4.38b, c, and d). Do half of your set, and then switch to counter-clockwise rotations for the remainder. Start with 10 reps on each side, and work your way up to 20 by adding 2 reps each week.

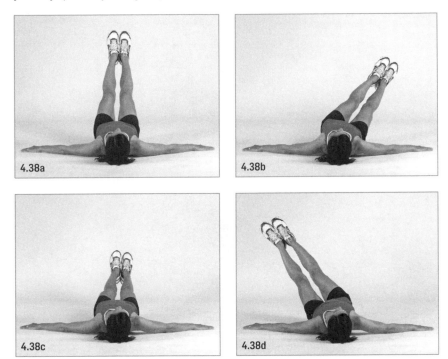

4.38a

4.38b

4.38c

4.38d

CORE

ONE-LEGGED HIP RAISE Start by lying face up with knees bent and feet flat on the floor. Stretch out your right leg and hold it just an inch or two in the air (4.39a). Keep your left knee bent and your left foot on the floor, and then push your hips up as high as you can (4.39b). Focus on keeping your right leg still as your hips rise; don't turn this into a leg raise by lifting your right leg up and down. Complete your set on one side, and then switch legs. Start with 10 reps on each side, and work your way up to 20 by adding 2 reps each week.

MUSCLE TARGET
Hamstrings

[+] ADVANCED For a *really* tough challenge, do one-legged hip raises with your planted foot on a medicine ball (4.40a and b). This unbalances your body, forcing your core to compensate, but mostly you'll feel your hamstrings working as they struggle to hold the ball steady throughout the movement.

CORE

ON A STABILITY BALL

SPREAD EAGLE Lie face down on the stability ball, with your feet on the floor, spread wide, and your body draped over the ball (4.41a). Hold arms in front of you, and raise your torso while keeping your feet on the floor (4.41b). Drop back down and repeat. Start with 20 reps, and add 5 each week until you reach 50.

MUSCLE TARGET
Lower back
Gluteus

4.41a

4.41b

REVERSE LEG RAISE From a prone position on the stability ball, roll forward until the ball is beneath your hips, with your hands on the floor (4.42a). Keeping your elbows locked and your arms straight, raise your legs up from your hips as high as you can (4.42b). Drop them back down and repeat. Start with 20 reps, and work your way up to 50 by adding 2 reps each week.

MUSCLE TARGET
Lower back
Gluteus

4.42a

4.42b

CORE

KNEE TUCK In plank position, put hands on the floor, arms straight and elbows locked, and tops of feet on the stability ball (4.43a). Keeping your hips as still as possible, bend your knees and roll the ball toward you, drawing your knees up toward your chest (4.43b). Start with 10 reps, and work your way up to 20 by adding 2 reps each week. To make this exercise more challenging, balance on your toes while keeping your feet as close together as possible.

4.43a

4.43b

CORE

CREATE YOUR PROGRAM

So now you have a good idea of the work you'll have to fit into your program, but having all the parts doesn't magically produce a program any more than having all the parts of a car makes it something you can drive. Just how does all this fit together?

To begin, you should have an idea of when you'll be doing any particular workout. The schedules in Chapter 9 will have suggestions on when to do your core work, but you can fit it almost anywhere in your schedule as long as you follow these guidelines:

- Do floor functional exercises at least *once per week.*
- Do standing functional exercises at least *twice per week.*
- Do balance work at least *twice per week.*
- Do jumps only *once per week.*
- Do some specific core work *every day* if possible or as often as is feasible.

Let's take a couple of typical days in a workout plan to see how this works. Assume it's Monday. You did your long run on Sunday, and you're planning out your day's routine. Because your legs are recovering from the run and you are a bit sore, you don't need to do your functional strength work today, and you certainly shouldn't do jumps. That leaves balance work and core work, which is completely appropriate.

Looking over your list of exercises, you decide to do 2 sets of each of the following exercises because you didn't do them in your last balance and core session:

- One-Legged Deadlift
- Standing Hurdle

You decide to do only these two balancing exercises because your legs don't feel up for doing lunges or squats. You can do those later in the week in your next balance workout. For core work, you decide to do these exercises:

- Windshield Wiper
- Roll-Up
- Crossover Crunch
- Side Crunch
- Side Hip Raise

And that's it. A total of 14 sets (2 each of 7 exercises), which shouldn't take you more than 20 minutes to do. That's your Monday balance and core workout.

On Tuesday, your legs are feeling more refreshed, and you decide to do all of your functional work, both standing and floor exercises. You also decide to do the following core exercises:

- Leg Raise
- Crunch
- Side Crunch
- Superman

Looking ahead, you've decided that on Wednesday you'll have to do some core work again, but you won't do any functional or balance work. On Thursday, you'll do jumps, functional floor work, and core, and on Friday you'll do balance, standing functional strength work, and core.

That's your week of functional and core work. As you can see, these routines can fit easily into and around your schedule. If you keep track of what you do, you also should be able to add enough variety to each workout to keep from getting bored.

5

Building a Runner's Body, Part 2
STRENGTH TRAINING AND WEIGHT LIFTING PROGRAM

RUNNING IS A TOTAL-BODY EXERCISE. The arms help drive leg turnover, powered by the shoulders, chest, and back, which together generate force and momentum, helping us to maintain balance as we move through space. Any deficiency along this chain of movement compromises the running motion, which can result in reduced running economy, strength, and endurance and even in injury. In order to improve as a runner, then, you need to do more than just strengthen your core. You need to get stronger throughout your entire body.

Weight lifting in particular performs a crucial function for runners: It helps to increase and maintain bone density. Bones are living tissue; they react to stress, just as muscles do, by either adapting or breaking down. Application of appropriate stress triggers the body to resculpt the bones so that they're capable of handling bigger loads, but running alone doesn't deliver the right amount of stress to the bones to trigger this adaptation. That's why so many runners suffer stress fractures at some point in their careers.

Strength training—and weight lifting in particular—can solve this problem. Even a minimal amount of regular strength training can help prevent the onset of stress fractures in the short term, as well as the onset of osteoporosis and loss of muscle mass in the long term. This is supported by research from the American College of Sports Medicine (ACSM), perhaps the most respected exercise information clearinghouse and teaching organization in the country. ACSM recommends that everyone perform some basic strength movements at least twice a week (Haskell et al. 2007).

Not all coaches consider weight lifting to be an essential part of a running program, however. They believe that to become a better runner, an athlete's first and only priority is to run. But a growing number of coaches have come to realize, as I have, that strength training is not only crucial to overall health and fitness but also fundamental to making progress as a runner.

A commonly voiced objection to strength training is that it adds unwanted bulk. That's simply wrong. For many people—especially lean runners—it would be hard to put on much bulk even if that were their goal. The strength training program presented here is designed to support running, not pack on muscle mass. No one can or will get big following this program.

So far, all of the exercises that we've reviewed—the running exercises, the balance work, squats, jumps, and core work—could be performed at home with no or minimal equipment. Many of the exercises that we'll now talk about can also be done this way. But some of them will require specialized gym equipment, such as weighted cables and strength training machines. These exercises are simply options, however, and aren't required. As I said earlier, no one is required to join a gym to follow this program, although having access to a gym will increase the range of choices. If belonging to a gym is not an option for you, however, simply cross out the exercises that you cannot do and focus on everything else. I promise you that your body will still get all the work it needs.

What *is* required, however, is a commitment to doing your strength training. As you'll see by the end of this chapter, these workouts won't take much of your time. But just because you won't be spending hours getting through each session doesn't mean they're less important than your other training sessions. Once you see and feel the results, you'll agree that these strength training workouts are well worth your time and effort.

THE STRENGTH AND WEIGHT LIFTING PROGRAM: THE THREE KEY ELEMENTS

Organized chaos might be the best way to describe what we'll be doing. But though this program might seem random and disjointed at first because there won't be a set exercise progression or rigid program to follow, within this disorder is a solid framework that forms the basis for all we do. In actuality, this is a very structured program that also allows for a great deal of flexibility and customization. The training program rests on three basic elements: your body's organization, pyramiding, and the power of two.

The Body's Organization

The first element concerns your body's organization. When we discussed aerobic exercise, we reviewed what occurs when runners hit the wall. When you are working anaerobically, however, muscle failure looks quite different. Here's a very quick biochemistry lesson (which I promise to make as brief and painless as possible).

The fuel for explosive anaerobic exercise is adenosine triphosphate (ATP), a compound stored in limited amounts in the mitochondria of each muscle cell. When you call upon a muscle to move quickly, the mitochondria in that muscle breaks down ATP into adenosine *di*phosphate, plus the released phosphate molecule and energy. There isn't very much ATP available in each cell, so when you've exhausted your supply—which can happen within a minute or so of intense work—you're done. Work comes to a halt.

But that's not the end of the story. Fuel used in anaerobic exercise can be quickly replenished after temporary muscle failure occurs (the opposite is the case in aerobic exercise). In fact, it can take place in just 30 seconds to a minute or so, depending on how hard you've worked. Think about it: Whenever you've exhausted yourself lifting something heavy—say, a piece of furniture or a box of books—you only needed a few moments of rest before you were able to get back to work.

Of course, anaerobic exhaustion of the muscles can't go on indefinitely; microdamage occurs to the muscle fibers as you work hard, which will eventually compromise the cell itself and bring work to a halt. But as we discussed earlier, the body responds to that damage by resculpting itself to handle those heavy loads, which is the entire point behind weight lifting and exercise.

This discussion helps explain why weight lifters break up their workouts into sets. Each hard set can last about a minute before deep fatigue sets in, which requires rest. But after a minute or so, the athlete can get right back to work.

Resting between sets can lead to a long workout, however. If you've ever been in gym during prime time, you can see the result: Of all the people in the workout room, few of them are actually exercising at any given moment. Probably not more than 10 percent. The rest of them are sitting around, waiting until they are recovered from their previous set.

For bodybuilders or powerlifters, it has to be this way because they are striving to push their muscles as far as possible in their gym workouts in order to trigger major mass-building adaptations. But as an endurance athlete, you don't need to push every major muscle so far; you just want to make sure all of them are strong enough to do their job adequately. For you, another approach is possible.

To understand the approach we're going to take, you need to understand how the body is organized. The human body can be visualized like Noah's Ark, with everything laid out in pairs. For every moving muscle, there's another muscle that opposes and supports it. Call these the agonist and antagonist. Whenever one muscle is working, its opposing number is resting.

This leads to a key insight: that rest and work among different muscle groups can take place at the same time. If we alternate the body parts being worked, we can work out continuously, giving each muscle group a chance to rest while the opposing group is working. The result is a workout that achieves our goals while taking half as much time.

Pyramiding

The second essential strength training element is pyramiding. This concept graphically describes a method for getting maximum results from a workout through the manipulation of resistance and repetitions. In order to discuss pyramiding, we first need to define some terms.

One-repetition max is any weight resistance level that is difficult enough to permit you to only perform one complete repetition with good form. Because this would by definition involve weight that is at the edge of your lifting capacity, this is an inherently dangerous set that should not be undertaken without an assistant (called a spotter).

One-rep-max sets are associated with powerlifting and bodybuilding because they tend to encourage the body to build mass and power rather than endurance. For this reason, the 1-rep max isn't of much use to runners, except generally as a guide to setting appropriate resistance levels, as we'll do in a moment.

A good alternative to doing the 1-rep max is to perform an exercise at a reduced resistance level—one that allows you to do 4–6 reps—and then guesstimate your 1-rep max from that level. Relative strength usually varies from person to person and even from body part to body, but as a rule of thumb, I've found that you can roughly calculate your 1-rep max by adding an extra 15 percent resistance to your 6-rep max.

Is this method entirely accurate? No. Is it a useful and safe way to gauge our strength limits? Yes.

Low resistance is any weight or resistance setting that is up to 60 percent of your 1-repetition max for a particular exercise. At this level, it is hard to gain much muscle mass, which makes this an ideal target range for endurance athletes.

High resistance is any weight or resistance that is 75–100 percent of your 1-repetition max. Exercises performed at this level will still encourage the body to build muscle size and power.

High repetition generally consists of 12 or more reps of an exercise performed to "temporary muscle failure," which is the point at which the muscles engaged in an exercise are too fatigued to continue working at the existing resistance level. Because we want to keep our exercise routine securely in the endurance-building arena and avoid building mass, we'll bump this up to 14–20 reps.

Low repetition consists of 8 reps or less of an exercise performed to temporary muscle failure. We'll adjust this figure upward to 10–14 reps in order to encourage endurance enhancement and not muscle mass improvement.

Low resistance/high repetition is any weight or resistance setting for an exercise that you can handle for 14 or more repetitions before you're too tired to continue. *High resistance/low repetition* is any weight or resistance setting for an exercise that you can handle only for 10–14 repetitions or less before you have to stop.

What's the real difference? High-rep/low-resistance exercises warm up a muscle and increase muscle endurance, creating lean muscle mass. A great example of this is, appropriately enough, running. Your body's movement through space during running includes hundreds or thousands of repetitions against very low resistance—essentially, the air and the ground—every time you work out.

Low-rep/high-resistance exercises, on the other hand, trigger gains in muscle size and strength. A great example of this is powerlifting, where athletes move heavily loaded barbells for a single repetition.

Both of these exercise modes provide valuable benefits for runners, when adjusted appropriately, because muscle strength provides explosive power and increases in bone density, while muscle endurance enables the body to engage in activity for longer periods of time. The trick is to figure out how to organize a workout so as to achieve both of these goals.

That's where pyramiding comes into play. Pyramiding describes the progression made from high repetition to low repetition and back again during the course of several sets of the same exercise. An initial high-repetition set would be considered the bottom of the pyramid, and a high-repetition set would be at the top.

Why start with a high-repetition set? Because a longer set will increase blood flow to a muscle group, warming it up and increasing its elasticity. This will safely prepare it for the heavier work that's to follow.

After the warm-up set, climb the pyramid by increasing the resistance and reducing the number of reps in order to work on strength. Finally, come back down the pyramid by cutting the resistance and doing 14–20 reps, which increases muscle endurance.

The Power of Two

The final essential strength training element concerns the most effective number of sets. Generally speaking, 2 sets of a given exercise provide the best bang for your fitness buck. Doing 1 set of an exercise provides significant and measurable health benefits over doing nothing at all. Doing 2 sets provides even greater benefits and allows for you to do both a high-rep and a low-rep set.

After 2 sets, however, the improvement curve flattens. Essentially, you get no more benefit from doing another set—unless you're the kind of person who just likes to spend all your free time in the gym. After 2 sets, you would be better off doing a different exercise rather than pressing ahead for a third or fourth set. That's because different exercises for the same muscle group work different cells within that muscle, so the greater variety of exercises that you do for a muscle, the more complete and balanced the muscle's development will be.

With all of these concepts under your belt, you're now ready to put your strength training program together. Bearing in mind these three key elements, here's how your program looks: You will start with a high-repetition set for each muscle group as a warm-up, alternating between opposing muscle groups as you go. Once you have warmed up those muscle groups, cycle through the exercises again at a higher resistance level, doing fewer repetitions for each. That will give you 2 sets per exercise, which is our goal.

But we're not done. Switch now to a different exercise for each muscle group, starting with a high-resistance/low-repetition set for each. After

THE STRENGTH AND WEIGHT LIFTING PROGRAM'S THREE KEY GUIDELINES

1. The pairing of muscle groups instructs us to move quickly from set to set during our workout. Think of this as alternating pushing and pulling exercises.
2. Pyramiding instructs us to include a high-repetition set and a low-repetition set for each exercise in order to get the best overall muscle development.
3. The power of two means that you gain the most benefit for your effort by performing 2 sets of each exercise. Instead of continuing with additional sets of the same exercise, you may then switch to a different related exercise.

completing those exercises, cycle through them again, switching to a low-resistance/high-repetition format. And that's the end of the workout.

Putting Together Your Strength and Weight Lifting Program

In the following pages you'll find lists of exercises for each major muscle group, organized into three categories: body-weight exercises, which involve no equipment and could be performed at home; free-weight exercises involving dumbbells or a medicine ball, which can also be performed at home; and cable and machine exercises, which generally can be performed only in a gym. For every workout, you'll choose from among these exercises.

Approach this list like it's a buffet, filling each workout with 2 exercises for each muscle group. Just take care to avoid choosing the same exercises for every workout. By rotating through all the available exercises in each category, you will have plenty of options (the "chaos" in our program) while fitting them within the framework we've developed (the "order").

Just remember that for every major muscle group, you'll do 2 exercises and that for every exercise, you'll do 2 sets: one low-resistance/high-repetition and one high-resistance/low-repetition. So as you move from set to set, there are two key questions you need to ask in order to make sure that you're on track:

1. *Have I used this muscle group before?* If the answer is no, then go high rep/low resistance because this is your warm-up set of your first exercise for this muscle. If the answer is yes, then go low rep/high resistance because this will be either the second set of your first exercise or the first set of the second exercise. In other words, the middle of the pyramid.

2. *Have I done this exercise before?* If the answer is yes, then simply do the opposite of what you did in the first set. So if you already did a high-rep/low-resistance set, then you are climbing the pyramid and need to go heavier. But if you already did your low-rep/high-resistance set, then you're descending the pyramid, and you need to switch to high rep/low resistance and work on your endurance.

By rotating muscle groups and sets this way, we turn the entire work-out into one big pyramid, making it the most time-efficient and effective strength building workout you'll ever get. Once you understand how it should flow, each session should take no more than 20–30 minutes, and be-cause it needs to be done only 2–3 times per week, this routine fits into even the busiest schedule.

Once you're familiar with all of the available options, you'll be able to ap-preciate that certain exercises stack well together into natural progressions. In a broad approach, you could organize your workout around modes. For example, you could do all your cable exercises together, rotating quickly from body part to body part. Similarly, you could put together a dumbbell routine or a machine routine. These types of workouts are especially useful when you have a very limited amount of time.

Focusing on the exercises themselves, you could aim to stack certain similar exercises together into progressions. For example, you could do all three dumbbell fly movements back-to-back and finish with low-reverse

STRENGTH TRAINING Q&A

Why not start with a lighter warm-up set for the second round of exercises? Even though these are new exercises for your workout, they're using muscles that you warmed up during the first round of exercises. Doing another warm-up set for these muscles would be a waste of your time and energy.

Will high-resistance exercises encourage muscle mass growth? For most people, real muscle growth comes from lifting heavy weights for 4–6 reps. Our low-rep/high-resistance sets consist of at least 10 repetitions, which is gener-ally too high to trigger much mass building. That said, if you have a body type that tends to put on mass easily, simply raise the repetition levels to 14 for the heavy set and 20 or more for the light set.

Why switch to different exercises midway through the workout? By switch-ing exercises, we work these muscles in a slightly different way, resulting in better overall development.

flys. Or you could alternate between push-ups and supermans or squats and deadlifts. These combinations work different muscle groups and effectively reduce the amount of time you would otherwise spend between exercises getting in position. This will enable you to have a more efficient and effective workout.

You could also do different exercises back-to-back that work the same muscle group, effectively doing one very long set. This technique is called a "superset." Another technique to make the most of your workout is to put together 2 or more exercises into combinations. As opposed to progressions, in which different exercises are performed in consecutive sets, combinations put them together in the same set. Each combination constitutes 1 repetition in that set. Two examples of combination exercises are squats with twisting one-arm shoulder press and push-ups with knee tucks.

STRENGTH AND WEIGHT LIFTING EXERCISES

In the world of fitness, there are hundreds, if not thousands, of different kinds of exercises, with new, trendy workout routines and pieces of equipment being marketed every year. But in reality, there are only four types of anaerobic exercises: body-weight, free-weight, cable, and machine. There are also a finite number of ways your body can move, roughly divided into pushing, pulling, and rotating actions. Almost every exercise you'll ever see or hear about is just a variation on themes that have existed for a long time.

This bit of knowledge makes the fitness world much more manageable. Even big fitness centers are actually surprisingly simple places once you understand how they're organized. Most of them are loaded with redundancy; it's often possible to perform the same exercise there in many ways.

Consider a rowing motion, for example. This exercise involves using the biceps and the muscles of the upper back to pull against resistance. In a typical gym, there might be anywhere from three to six ways to do this movement. You could hold onto a stationary bar or strap system and pull yourself forward (a body-weight exercise), use a seated rowing station (a machine exercise), put a knee and a hand on a bench and do a dumbbell row (a free-weight exercise), or do one- or two-handed cable rows (a cable exercise). You

TABLE 5.1

EXERCISE MODES

EXERCISE MODE	CORE ENGAGEMENT	EASE OF ALTERING RESISTANCE	SAFETY
BODY WEIGHT	X		X
FREE WEIGHT	X	X	
CABLE	X	X	
MACHINE		X	X

wouldn't need to do all of these exercises in any given workout; you could just choose one of them to check off your rowing exercise.

That doesn't mean that all of those rowing exercises are exactly the same, however. Each mode provides a slightly different benefit and also harbors some small drawback. Table 5.1 compares the different modes of performing a movement like rowing.

Body-weight exercises engage the core and are generally very safe because you will never be moving very large amounts of weights. But because you are using only your own body without any additional equipment, it's hard to change the resistance levels. Some exercises can be made more difficult by altering your position or the speed of the repetitions, but there are still absolute limits.

Although it is possible to increase resistance on body-weight exercises by holding weights or placing them on your body for different movements, I don't consider this to be safe in many instances, and it is certainly not necessary to improve muscle endurance. So instead of increasing resistance here, go slow and slower instead, taking 5–10 seconds for each part of the movement. Afterward, return to regular speed for the high-repetition sets.

Free-weight exercises can engage the core. Using dumbbells can also work your muscles more completely because you will have to work hard to balance the weights in space. If you think of your body as a chain with each end bolted to the floor, you can see why these are often referred to as *open-*

chain exercises, as one end of the chain—the part of your body holding the weight—isn't tethered to the ground.

Free-weight exercises allow for quick changes in resistance because you can simply grab a different set of dumbbells. But perhaps the best feature of free weights is the ease of movement, which allows for great creativity. You can do a great many exercises and even invent some of your own. But the downside of this freedom is that if you're not careful to use proper form, you can easily hurt yourself.

Cable exercises allow for easy changes in resistance, with almost as much freedom of movement as that provided by free weights. Cable work also tends to involve the core. But even though cables are marginally safer to use than free weights because they can more easily be picked up and put down, injury is still possible if you don't maintain proper form.

Machines provide a very safe environment in which to exercise. As long as you keep your body on the pads and do the exercise as intended, it's difficult to get injured. Also, changing resistance is usually as easy as moving a pin from one setting on the machine's weight stack to another. One downside to working on machines, however, is the lack of room for creativity. Most machines can move only in a single way, facilitating one or two movements. Another drawback is the lack of core engagement while working machines.

The answer for us is not to choose among these exercises but to incorporate all of them into your routine so that you can get all of the benefits from each while minimizing their downsides.

Keep in mind that all of these training modes are complementary. In fact, to a large extent, all of the drills, balance and core work, and strength and weight lifting exercises are overlapping. Balance exercises, for example, rely on the transverse abdominus and, often, muscles of the hips and inner and outer leg. Some of our strength training also works the core, as do our drills, which also work specific muscle groups, just as in strength training.

By including all of these modes in this program, we build fitness in several ways, resulting in stronger, healthier bodies that can more easily handle the stresses of high-intensity training with fewer injuries while delivering speed on race day.

In order to get the most from your workout, there are two more guidelines to keep in mind when choosing exercises. First, *choose complex over simple movements.* The more joints you get moving during an exercise, the more muscles you'll activate to move all those body parts. If you want to do the most efficient workout possible, then focus mostly on multi-joint movements instead of single-joint movements. That's why you won't find any arm exercises in this program. The arms get worked anyway when you do most of the chest, shoulder, and back exercises. (There is nothing wrong with single-joint exercises. You'll find some of these in my program, such as shoulder and chest flys. But as a rule of thumb, keep it complex.)

Second, *destabilize when possible.* Any time that you have to work at staying balanced, you work your core. To get the most benefit from every exercise, then, look for ways to destabilize your base. If an exercise calls for you to sit or lie on a bench, try a stability ball instead. If you're supposed to stand during an exercise, stand on one foot for half the set and then switch to the other or stand on either side of a BOSU.

Be creative, and do whatever you can to safely shake things up, but remember to be safe, especially when using free weights. Do not put yourself in awkward positions, and do not make any quick, jerky moves. The freedom you have with free weights is exercised at your peril if you aren't careful.

Now that you know more about strength training and weight lifting theory than most people you'll ever meet in a gym, it's time to review your exercises menu. For each muscle group, I have added exercises in the four modes. Don't think of this as an exhaustive list, however; if you observe a new exercise at the gym or read about one in a reputable fitness magazine, feel free to add it to your routine where appropriate.

GROUP 1: CHEST

BODY WEIGHT

MUSCLE TARGET

Pecs

Delts

Triceps

Abs

PUSH-UP Start on hands and knees, and hold your body rigid in a straight line from knees to shoulders (5.1a). Keeping your chin up, lower down until your nose is almost touching the floor (5.1b), and then slowly lift up again. When you can do 10 of these, try to do them from your toes. When you can do 10 from your toes, add 2 reps each week until you can do 30.

MUSCLE TARGET

Pecs

Delts

Triceps

Abs

[+] ADVANCED To make it harder, put your hands on a stability ball and do incline push-ups, and then turn around and put your feet on the ball and do push-ups (5.2a and b). Using a BOSU is also an option. Place your BOSU soft side down with your hands on its solid side, and do push-ups from that position.

STRENGTH

FREE WEIGHT

DUMBBELL CHEST PRESS Lying back on a bench or stability ball, lower a pair of dumbbells until they're even with your chest, with your hands out past your armpits (5.3a). Press them upward, slowly arcing them together until they touch at the top of the movement (5.3b). Add intensity by doing this exercise unilaterally, with a single dumbbell, alternating sides with each set. This will push your abs to work harder to keep you from toppling over. Start with 10 reps, add 2 reps each week until you reach 20, and then increase the weight and start back at 10 and work your way up.

MUSCLE TARGET
Pecs
Delts
Abs
Triceps

5.3a

5.3b

[+] ADVANCED This exercise focuses more on the upper chest and anterior deltoids than the chest press above. Perform the same movement as for the Dumbbell Chest Press, but with a bench set at an incline or against a stability ball while sitting closer to the ground (5.4a and b). Start with 10 reps, and add 2 reps each week until you reach 20, and then increase the weight and start back at 10 and work your way up.

MUSCLE TARGET
Pecs
Delts
Triceps

5.4a

5.4b

STRENGTH

CABLE AND MACHINE

MUSCLE TARGET
Pecs
Delts
Abs

CABLE CROSSOVER This is a simple exercise, working only the shoulder joint, but you can still activate your core muscles by doing it unilaterally. Standing off to the side of the cable machine, with the handgrip set at a high level (5.5a), bring your arm sweeping down across your body (5.5b). Keep elbow bent and held high throughout the movement, and then switch to the other side. Start with 10 reps, and add 2 reps each week until you reach 20, and then increase the resistance and start back at 10 and work your way up.

MUSCLE TARGET
Pecs
Delts
Abs

CABLE SCOOP This exercise is similar to the Cable Crossover, but with the handle set at a low level (5.6a). Sweep your arm up and across your body (5.6b), and then switch to the other side. Start with 10 reps, and add 2 reps each week until you reach 20, and then increase the weight and start back at 10 and work your way up.

STRENGTH

CABLE PUNCH This complex exercise uses the shoulder and elbow joints and involves torso rotation. Set the handle slightly higher than shoulder level, and grip it with your right hand (5.7a). With your left leg in front and right leg behind, keeping your elbow up, throw a controlled punch while holding the cable (5.7b). Rotate your torso to reach out as far as possible. Finish the set and repeat it with your left hand, setting your right leg in front of you. Start with 10 reps, and add 2 reps each week until you reach 20, and then increase the resistance and start back at 10 and work your way up.

MUSCLE TARGET
Pecs
Delts
Triceps
Abs

MACHINE SEATED CHEST PRESS Your hands should be at armpit level, with elbows raised so that forearms are parallel to the ground (5.8a). Slowly reach out as far as possible (5.8b) and then return. Avoid letting the weights touch down on the stack because that relieves pressure and allows an unnecessary rest time. Start with 10 reps, and add 2 reps each week until you reach 20, and then increase the resistance and start back at 10 and work your way up.

MUSCLE TARGET
Pecs
Delts
Triceps

STRENGTH

MUSCLE TARGET
Pecs
Delts
Triceps

MACHINE INCLINE PRESS Similar to the Machine Seated Chest Press, this exercise will have you pushing handles away from your body, but at a slightly upward trajectory (5.9a and b). This puts more stress on the upper part of the chest and the anterior deltoids. Because these muscles are smaller than the larger pectoral muscles, expect to be able to use 20–30 percent less resistance here than on the Chest Press. Do not to rush this exercise, and as with the Chest Press, avoid letting the weights drop between repetitions. Start with 10 reps, and add 2 reps each week until you reach 20, and then increase the resistance and start back at 10 and work your way up.

5.9a   5.9b

PEC-DECK STATION This machine will require you to sit down with your back to the weight stack and reach out to the movable arms on either side of you (5.10a). Depending on the design of the machine, you will find pads on which you should place your forearm or handles to grip. Lean back against the pad, bring the machine arms all the way together, and hold that position for 2 seconds (5.10b). Extend your arms until you feel a comfortable stretch across your chest, but avoid reaching too far back, as that puts the shoulder joint at risk.

   This is a single-joint exercise—working only the shoulder joint—so it won't involve as many muscle groups as the Chest Press, which also engages the elbow joints and triceps muscles. Nevertheless, this exercise works the chest in a way that the pressing exercise doesn't and provides a nice stretch to boot. Start with 10 reps, and add 2 reps each week until you reach 20, and then increase the resistance and start back at 10 and work your way up.

MUSCLE TARGET
Pecs
Delts

5.10a

5.10b

STRENGTH

GROUP 2: BACK

BODY WEIGHT

<table>
<tr><td>MUSCLE TARGET</td></tr>
<tr><td>Lats</td></tr>
<tr><td>Traps</td></tr>
<tr><td>Biceps</td></tr>
</table>

PULL-UP Hang from an overhead bar (5.11a), and pull your body up until your face clears the bar (5.11b), and then lower yourself back down and repeat. Alternate between using a wide overhand grip and a narrow underhand grip to engage as much of the lat muscles as possible. Keep your legs straight, and don't let your body swing back and forth during the exercise. Start with as many as you can, making sure that you don't swing or curl up your body to force out that last rep, and work your way up to 10 reps.

5.11a

5.11b

FREE WEIGHT

DUMBBELL DEADLIFT Stand a dumbbell on one end on the floor, gripping the top end with both hands. Keep your pelvis tilted back and your backside sticking out, with your back arched and your knees locked in a slightly bent position (5.12a). Now stand up and lift the dumbbell (5.12b). Start with 10 reps, increase to 14, and then graduate to heavier weight. This is an excellent exercise for building strength in the hips, lower back, and legs, but make sure you use proper form at all times.

MUSCLE TARGET
Gluteus
Lower back

5.12a   5.12b

DUMBBELL ROW Bend over, with one hand on a bench or stability ball for support (5.13a), and pull a dumbbell up to your ribcage (5.13b). Drop down again and repeat. Start with 10 reps, and add 2 reps each week until you reach 14, and then increase the weight and start back at 10 and work your way up.

MUSCLE TARGET
Lats
Traps
Biceps

5.13a   5.13b

STRENGTH

MUSCLE TARGET
Abs

DUMBBELL TWISTING SWING Stand with your legs close together, holding a dumbbell with both hands. Starting with the dumbbell near your outer hip (5.14a), swing the dumbbell widely across to your other side, keeping arms as straight as possible (5.14b). Follow the dumbbell with your eyes, and rotate your shoulders as you do the movement. Imagine that you're a home-run hitter swinging for the fences. Repeat from the other side. Start with 10 reps, and add 2 reps each week until you reach 14, and then increase the weight and start back at 10 and work your way up.

MUSCLE TARGET
Triceps

Upper back

DUMBBELL SWINGBACK Bend over, with one hand on a stability ball for support (5.15a). Hold a dumbbell with your other hand and keeping your arm straight, swing your arm back toward your side as high as possible (5.15b). Imagine that you're bowling and swinging a ball back. Start with 10 reps, and add 2 reps each week until you reach 14, and then increase the weight and start back at 10 and work your way up.

DUMBBELL LOW REVERSE FLY Hold a pair of dumbbells at thigh level (5.16a). Bending slightly, swing your arms outward to your side, keeping them as wide as possible (5.16b). Imagine that you're trying to touch your elbows together behind your back. Start with 10 reps, and add 2 reps each week until you reach 14, and then increase the weight and start back at 10 and work your way up.

MUSCLE TARGET

Rhomboids

Traps

CABLE AND MACHINE

CABLE PULL-DOWN This movement is simply the cable version of a pull-up, so do it the same way, alternating between a wide (5.17a and b) and a narrow grip. Start with 10 reps, and add 2 reps each week until you reach 20, and then increase the weight and start back at 10 and work your way up.

MUSCLE TARGET

Lats

Traps

Biceps

STRENGTH

MUSCLE TARGET

Lats

Traps

Biceps

Abs

TWISTING ONE-ARM CABLE PULL This exercise is similar to the Cable Punch, except instead of pushing against the cable, you pull. Alternate between setting the cable at the high (5.18a and b) and low (5.19a and b) positions, and give yourself plenty of room. Start with 10 reps, and add 2 reps each week until you reach 20, and then increase the weight and start back at 10 and work your way up.

STRENGTH

MACHINE ROW Be sure to keep your body firmly against the pad so as to protect your lower back (5.20a). Pull the handles back toward your ribcage (5.20b) and slowly return. Start with 10 reps, and add 2 reps each week until you reach 20, and then increase the weight and start back at 10 and work your way up.

MUSCLE TARGET
Lats
Traps
Biceps

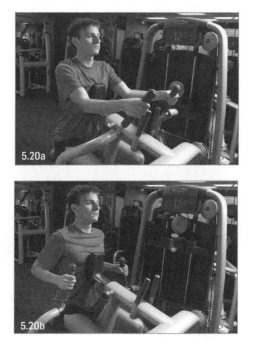

GROUP 3: SHOULDERS

FREE WEIGHT

All of these exercises are performed from a standing position.

DUMBBELL SHOULDER PRESS Hold your body straight; do not lean or sway. Start by holding a single dumbbell with an overhand grip at approximately ear level, with your palm facing forward (5.21a). Raise the dumbbell up, but don't lock your elbow (5.21b). Switch to the other side and repeat. Start with 10 reps, and add 2 reps each week until you reach 20, and then increase the weight and start back at 10 and work your way up.

5.21a

5.21b

STRENGTH

DUMBBELL FRONT RAISE Hold a pair of dumbbells in front of your body near your lap, with your palms facing toward your body (5.22a). Keeping your arms straight, raise them in front of you to eye level (5.22b). Lower and repeat. Start with 10 reps, and add 2 reps each week until you reach 20, and then increase the weight and start back at 10 and work your way up.

MUSCLE TARGET
Delts

5.22a 5.22b

DUMBBELL LATERAL RAISE This is similar to the Dumbbell Front Raise, except you raise the dumbbells out to your sides. Start with 10 reps, and add 2 reps each week until you reach 20, and then increase the weight and start back at 10 and work your way up. To make this more challenging, stand on one leg while performing this exercise (5.23a and b).

MUSCLE TARGET
Delts

5.23a 5.23b

STRENGTH

MUSCLE TARGET
Delts

DUMBBELL HIGH REVERSE FLY This exercise is trickier than the other two fly movements because it shifts through several planes and alters the body's center of gravity. Avoid swaying. Hold the dumbbells, palms inward toward the body (5.24a). Swing the dumbbells outward, flipping your hands so that your palms face away from you (5.24b). Start with 10 reps, and add 2 reps each week until you reach 20, and then increase the weight and start back at 10 and work your way up.

MUSCLE TARGET
Delts

Lower back

Hip flexors

Hamstrings

DUMBBELL FRONT SWING Holding a single dumbbell with both hands, do a deadlift, keeping your back arched, your backside sticking out, and your knees slightly bent (5.25a). After straightening up, continue lifting the weight until you've swung it up over your head (5.25b). Lower and repeat. Start with 10 reps, and add 2 reps each week until you reach 20, and then increase the weight and start back at 10 and work your way up.

DUMBBELL SHRUG Hold a pair of heavy dumbbells at your sides, with your palms facing inward (5.26a). Keeping arms perfectly straight, shrug your shoulders to lift up the dumbbells as high as you can (5.26b). Start with 10 reps, and add 2 reps each week until you reach 20, and then increase the weight and start back at 10 and work your way up.

MUSCLE TARGET
Traps

Rhomboids

DUMBBELL PULLOVER Lie face up on a bench—or, for a greater challenge, a stability ball—and hold a single dumbbell with both hands over your body (5.27a). Swing the dumbbell back up over your head toward the floor, going as far as you can comfortably go (5.27b). As an alternative, instead of using one dumbbell, you can hold a lighter dumbbell in each hand. Start with 10 reps, and add 2 reps each week until you reach 20, and then increase the weight and start back at 10 and work your way up.

MUSCLE TARGET
Delts

Upper back

STRENGTH

CABLE AND MACHINE

MUSCLE TARGET

Delts

Triceps

SEATED MACHINE SHOULDER PRESS Adjust the seat height so that the handles will be at your ear level. Sit down and remember to keep your lower back firmly pressed against the seat (5.28a). Do not arch your back to gain leverage; this will only strain your lower back. Press the handles upward until your arms are mostly straight, although you should avoid locking your elbows, as this will just stress the joint and relieve the pressure on the muscles (5.28b). Start with 10 reps, and add 2 reps each week until you reach 20, and then increase the resistance and start back at 10 and work your way up.

5.28a

5.28b

GROUP 4: LEGS

BODY WEIGHT

SQUATS AND LUNGES Most of the body-weight legwork that you should do was reviewed in the sections on lunges and jumps in Chapter 4, as well as the section on running drills in Chapter 2. Do these exercises at least once per week. For squats and lunges, start with one set of 10 reps and add 2 reps each week until you reach 20; then go to two sets of 10 reps and work your way up to two sets of 20.

FREE WEIGHT

MONKEY SQUAT Stand with feet slightly wider than shoulder-width apart, and hold a single heavy dumbbell directly below you (5.29a). Keep your back arched and hips rotated as you look straight ahead. Squat down but do not allow your knees to go past your toes (5.29b). Aim to do sets of 20 repetitions, and when the dumbbell you use feels very manageable, increase the resistance by 5-pound increments.

MUSCLE TARGET
Hamstrings
Quads
Gluteus
Abs

5.29a

5.29b

STRENGTH

CABLE AND MACHINE

MUSCLE TARGET

Hamstrings

Quads

Gluteus

LEG PRESS This exercise is performed on machines that are either platform based, in which you sit on a stationary seat and push a weighted platform away from you, or sled based, in which the platform is stationary and you push your seat back along a pair of rails (5.30a and b). Aim to do sets of 20 repetitions, and increase the resistance by 10-pound increments when the exercise starts to feel easily manageable. Just as with the squats, all the major muscle groups of the legs are engaged here, including the hamstrings, quads, and glutes, but if you place your feet lower on the platform, you'll put more pressure on the hamstrings, whereas if you place your feet higher on the platform, you'll put more pressure on the quads. Aim to get a bit of both by alternating the way in which you do this exercise.

STRENGTH

LEG EXTENSION This exercise involves sitting in a chairlike machine and pushing up against a roller that lies across the front of your ankles (5.31a). Keeping firmly in your seat and using the handgrips or belt that might be available, slowly raise and lower the weighted roller (5.31b).

MUSCLE TARGET
Quads

This is a good strength builder for important running muscles, but deep flexion or extension can put an unsafe amount of pressure on the knees, so be sure not to lock out your knees or drop your legs down all the way while doing this exercise. Start with 14 repetitions, and increase by 2 repetitions per week until you reach 20; then increase the resistance by 10 pounds, and start over again with 14 repetitions.

5.31a

5.31b

STRENGTH

ABDUCTOR AND ADDUCTOR MACHINES These are seated machines in which you position your legs in weighted, padded leg rests and either spread your legs apart for abduction (5.33a and b) or bring them together for adduction (5.34a and b) against resistance in order to work the inner and outer thigh muscles. Start with 14 repetitions, and increase by 2 repetitions per week until you reach 20; then increase the resistance by 10 pounds, and start over again with 14 repetitions.

MUSCLE TARGET
Abductors

5.33a

5.33b

MUSCLE TARGET
Adductors

5.34a

5.34b

STRENGTH

CABLE LEG SWING With the cable at the setting closest to the floor, place your foot into the padded sleeve and position it around your ankle. Keeping your leg straight, swing it laterally against resistance to work your outer hip and abductors (5.35a and b) or swing inward across your body to work your adductors (5.36a and b). Start with 14 repetitions, and increase by 2 repetitions per week until you reach 20; then increase the resistance by 5 pounds, and start over again with 14 repetitions.

MUSCLE TARGET

Hip flexors

Abductors

MUSCLE TARGET

Adductors

STRENGTH

CREATE YOUR PROGRAM

Now that you are familiar with your strength and weight lifting options, let's examine what a single training session might look like. Recall what modes of training you worked on in the previous training session. Remember that you'll achieve best results by varying the modes of training, so if your previous workout involved dumbbells, choose machines or body-weight exercises. Or if you mixed the modes of training in your previous workout, you should now choose just one mode for each body part. Remember: You should plan to do a strength and weight lifting workout *two to three times per week.*

Let's walk through a possible training day to see how this works. Assume that you last did a routine that focused on cable and machine exercises. That leaves free-weight and body-weight exercises for your next workout. As you look at the proposed routine below, keep in mind that this is only one of many possible workouts that would have been appropriate. Notes in parentheses explain some of the reasoning behind the exercise choices.

- Dumbbell Chest Press, 20 repetitions using light weight
- Pull-Up, wide grip, 10 repetitions
- Dumbbell Chest Press, advanced, 14 repetitions using heavy weight
- Pull-Up, narrow grip, 10 repetitions
- Dumbbell Chest Press, 14 repetitions using heavy weight (At this point you might want to do a second set of wide and narrow grip pull-ups, but you know from past experience that you won't be able to do at least 10 repetitions of either exercise, so you move onto another back exercise instead.)
- Dumbbell Row, 14 repetitions using heavy weight
- Dumbbell Shoulder Press, 14 repetitions using heavy weight. (Even though this is the first shoulder exercise, the deltoids are already warmed up from the chest work.)
- Dumbbell Pullover, 14 repetitions using heavy weight
- Monkey Squat, 20 repetitions using light weight
- Dumbbell Row, 20 repetitions using light weight
- Dumbbell Chest Press, advanced, 20 repetitions using light weight

- Dumbbell Low Reverse Fly, 14 repetitions using heavy weight
- Monkey Squat, 14 repetitions using heavy weight
- Dumbbell Shoulder Press, 20 repetitions using light weight
- Dumbbell Low Reverse Fly, 20 repetitions using light weight
- Dumbbell Pullover, 20 repetitions using light weight

And that's it. Just as with the sample core workout routine we reviewed in Chapter 4, this workout consists of a total of 16 sets (2 each of 8 exercises), which should take you approximately 20–25 minutes to do. Looking ahead, your next workout may consist of push-ups, machines, or cable machine exercises, or a combination of all available options.

6

Putting It All Together

NOW IT'S TIME TO TAKE ALL THESE IDEAS AND PLANS and put them into practice. The first step is to pick a race. Then you'll write out your training program (with assistance from the charts in Chapter 9) and, finally, plan out your racing strategy. Although a good plan doesn't guarantee a perfect race, it would be hard to run a perfect race without one.

TARGET YOUR RACE

Figuring out which race you want to aim for involves a number of considerations. Race conditions, course, and race dates are three key factors to keep in mind.

What race conditions do you prefer? Every runner has racing preferences. Under what kinds of race conditions do you perform best? Cool weather—in the low 50s or high 40s—is favored by many runners, but your own preference may differ. With marathons available almost all year, you should have no problem finding a race that appeals to you.

Of course, you never know what you might get on race day. Put the odds in your favor by researching what the race-day conditions have been over the previous five years.

What kind of course do you like? Some people love a pancake-flat course, whereas others find that sort of course mind-numbingly dull and prefer a mix of hills. Some runners find that they have a talent for big hills and like to find races where that will give them an edge over other competitors.

There's also more to consider than the course itself. The major marathons have 20,000 or more participants, with tens of thousands of spectators lining the course and music stages set up every few miles along the way. For some, this is the ideal experience, whereas others perform best in a rural race with a small number of participants and few spectators.

Which race dates work best with your other obligations? Racing doesn't exist in a vacuum. We all have work and social obligations that need our attention. And that's how it should be; if running took top priority over everything in your life, rather than playing its important but limited role, that would be a sign of imbalance.

Identify as many likely unavailable weekends in your coming year as possible. Many businesses are partly seasonal, and many family and social get-togethers are well known and predictable. Figure out which race weekends are simply nonstarters.

Once you've cross-referenced all of your information, eliminated unavailable weekends, and circled realistic possibilities, you're ready to narrow your choices down to just a few. Any racing schedule can be sidetracked by unexpected events. My grandmother liked to say that we make plans and God laughs. So designate one of these choices as your primary goal race and the others as back-ups.

Finally, count backward from your target race weekend for the number of weeks you will be training (refer to the sample programs contained in Chapter 9 to get this number). This is your training cycle for your target race.

WRITE DOWN YOUR GOALS

Before you can put together a training schedule, you'll have to set a realistic goal for your target race. Race goals can be either process- or result-oriented. An example of a *process goal* would be to develop and stick to a good race-day hydration and fueling plan. For process goals, success is measured by taking all the steps you committed to taking, regardless of what your finishing time turns out to be—although, of course, taking all the right steps along the way puts the odds in your favor of reaching a good finishing time.

A *result goal* is concerned only with a specific race finish time. Even though it relies on all those steps that get you to the finish line, your result goal doesn't care whether you successfully hit all your process goals along the way. If you didn't arrive at the finish line when you planned to, even if you hit all of your process goals, you failed to hit this goal. It's not about the journey; it's about the destination.

To put together a training plan, you need both process and results goals, but the result goal comes first because all of your workouts will be keyed off that time. You will use that finishing time to set a training pace for your speed, tempo, and long run workouts.

Don't take this step lightly. Training for a race without setting a result goal is like getting dressed in the morning without having any idea what the weather will be; you might get lucky and end up ok, but don't bet on it.

Your result goal should be based on your race times at all distances over the previous two years. If you haven't raced within that time frame, you can do your own race now. Race a 5K, which is 3.1 miles, on a treadmill or a track. (For your reference, doing a 5K on a track equals approximately 12.3 laps.) Aim to run at a high effort level—an 8 on the RPE.

Once you have your race numbers together, calculate a realistic target race goal by referring to the pace chart in Appendix A. Remember that any single number will represent a bit of guessing and wishful thinking as you factor in past training, race conditions, and finishing times. Of course, the longer you've been running and the more races you've run, the more grounded in reality your goal will be.

The best way to set a race goal is to work off of your finishing times in prior races at that distance. If you're using shorter races to set your goals, however, you have to factor in your need to run a slower pace for longer races. You can't race a marathon at your 5K pace, for example, and you would crash badly if you tried to do so.

Still, you could use your finishing times in shorter races as a guideline for setting a goal for a longer race. Working this out is as much art as science, but as a rough rule of thumb, expect to add 1 minute per mile to your 5K time when calculating a half-marathon goal pace, and 1 minute 15 seconds if moving up to the marathon. If you're using the 10K as your predictor, add 30 seconds for a half-marathon goal pace and 45 seconds for a marathon. When moving from the half-marathon to the marathon, add 30 seconds per mile.

One way to test whether your race goals are realistic is to periodically run shorter races during the course of your training. Not only will this give you important feedback, but it will also inject a bit more variety and fun into your training. A speed workout or a tempo run could be substituted with a 5K, 10K, or 10-mile race without causing a disruption to your program. You may find that you were too ambitious in setting your goals, or perhaps—and this happens more often than you might guess—you'll find that you are running better than you thought you would and that you should set your sights a bit higher.

WRITE YOUR TRAINING PROGRAM

Now you're ready to take a training plan from this book out onto the road. In Chapter 9 you'll find six training programs—three each for the half-marathon and the marathon. For each of these race distances, there are intermediate, advanced, and competitive programs. The simplest approach is to assess which category you belong in and use the appropriate program as written. If you haven't run a marathon or half-marathon previously or haven't run any races within the previous two years, this is your best approach.

If you do have some racing history, however, you can tweak the program to address your strengths and weaknesses. If endurance is your strong suit, then substitute additional speed work for two monthly long workouts. If your speed is relatively stronger, you can do two fewer tempo runs or speed workouts per month and add two more long endurance sessions.

You can also expand the schedule to add additional weeks of training if your base of speed and endurance together isn't as strong as you would like it to be. And because the programs recommend specific strength training modes, you can adjust them to take into account which modes you may not have access to (such as a gym and particular strength training machines) or which ones you prefer.

In other words, the training schedules in Chapter 9 are recommendations, not orders. But if you make changes, make sure that those changes are based on objective fact, not on a reluctance to do certain parts of the program. As I said in Chapter 2, to get the most from this program, you need to commit to all of it, not just the parts you may already like, be good at, or are familiar with.

RUN YOUR BEST POSSIBLE RACE

Once you've targeted your race, done all your training, and made it to the starting line, all you need to do is run the race you've prepared for. If you can do that, you'll get the result you want. Simple, right? Think again.

Jim Hage, a back-to-back two-time winner of the Marine Corps Marathon (1988 and 1989), three-time Olympic Trials Marathon qualifier with an 8th place finish in the 1992 Trials, and owner of a 2:15 marathon PR, once told me that of the approximately 80 marathons he had run, he ran a negative split—running the second half of his race faster than the first—only once in what turned out to be his PR race. In all his other marathons, he went out faster than he had planned. "I just kept thinking all those times that maybe it was my day for a great race," he said. If a runner of the caliber of Jim Hage has trouble sticking to his race plan, you know that this is no simple task.

Decide on Your Race Pace

The most efficient way to run a race is to throw down even splits, running each mile at a nearly identical pace. Most professional and elite runners aim to run negative splits, in which they pick up the pace slightly in the second half of the race. Being able to pick up the pace late in a race shows that you ran the first half controlled and within your ability, leaving you with plenty of fuel to finish strong.

The key to running a negative split is to refrain from going out too fast in the beginning, despite the excitement of race day and how wonderful you might feel. This is crucial. When you run too fast early on, you set yourself up for a possible implosion later. That's because almost every runner who slows down in a race does so because his or her body offers no other choice. Once your body is in distress, it just wants to stop.

The only way to avoid that dire situation is to run the race you've prepared for, which means running at a pace that your tempo runs, endurance base, and speed workout have prepared you to hold for the complete race distance. By race day, you know exactly what this pace is because you've been basing all of your training around it.

You made a deal with your body during training, preparing your body to run a certain kind of race. If you ask it to run faster, it will burn through fuel stores quicker than a spark in a gunpowder factory.

Is there ever a time to take a chance during a race? The answer is a cautious "yes." If weather conditions are ideal and you are feeling especially strong and well prepared, you could take a calculated gamble and try to push your pace slightly. You might wind up with a great race. But keep in mind that if things go wrong, you might have to drop out instead. That's ok. There's nothing wrong with taking a calculated risk and failing.

The key, however—and this is important—is to drop out of your race as soon as you get in serious stress and start to slow down. Once your body starts putting on the brakes, forcing it onward will only cause greater muscle damage, which will require a longer recovery time. By dropping out before too much harm has been done, you keep open the option of retooling your program to target one of your back-up races.

Climb Every Mountain

A good race plan includes knowledge of the racecourse. Although perfectly even mile splits are ideal, few racecourses allow for that kind of regularity. If there's a big hill on the course, not only would it be hard to maintain your pace going uphill, but also attempting to do so would burn more energy than it would be worth. A better strategy is to plan to slow a bit on the hill and make it up with a slightly faster pace on the downhill or to bank a cushion of time earlier in the race that you could give away on the hill. In either case, you should adjust your pace so that you're using the same amount of energy throughout. This is referred to as "even effort" pacing, which is appropriate

WHEN ENOUGH IS ENOUGH

How do you know when enough is enough? If you knew your blood chemistry, you could monitor your blood sugar (glycogen) levels as well as your lactic acid levels. But because that won't happen, you'll need to monitor some other factors instead. Slowing down dramatically—by a minute or more per mile—can be a sign that your muscle function is compromised by microtears, which could soon turn into more serious damage. Cramping and excessive muscle soreness are other signs, although these factors are more subjective. And, of course, any sign of an actual injury—a sharp pain in a muscle or sudden pain in a joint—is reason enough to call it a day.

Even though this all makes logical sense, when the moment comes, most runners naturally find it hard to drop out. If you want to race your best, however, you need to commit to not just training smart but also racing smart. This is a part of racing that most nonrunners don't understand. When Paula Radcliffe dropped out of the Olympic Marathon in Sydney in 2004, the British press raked her over the coals for being a quitter, despite her having won scores of other races and having owned the women's marathon world record. I have no doubt that Paula gave the race everything she had, but once she saw that it was not her day, there was no point in continuing to run. As a professional, she needed to protect her body, which, after all, was her single greatest asset.

Commit yourself to being smarter than you are brave.

for very hilly courses. If you maintain an even effort, you will be able to maintain the same RPE on the uphills as on the downhills.

Whenever you approach a hill on a racecourse, think back to all of the hills you ran in training and remind yourself that you are fully prepared and ready for any hill the race throws at you. Don't let the hill intimidate you. More importantly, don't let the published race elevation intimidate you. Most hills look more ferocious on paper than on the ground because the distance is shrunk on the chart, often making elevation changes seem more dramatic than they are.

Whenever you are on a hill, closely monitor your form as you ascend it. Remind yourself to maintain a tall running posture, to swing your arms smoothly from the shoulders, and to shorten your stride as the pitch increases. On the back side of the hill, remember to lean forward as you glide down, taking short, quick steps.

Sound familiar? It should. By race day, you will have been doing this kind of running for months. Keep reminding yourself of that fact.

Bear in mind as well that hills can be your friend if you know how to use them. If you're racing against another runner in a real competition or just engaging in a mind game for a bit of motivation, you can use the hill to make your move to pass him or her.

To do so, stay close to your rival as you approach the hill, maintaining a position just a step or two behind as you ascend. As your rival clears the top, he or she will likely slow for a moment to regroup, using that pause to recoup energy and take a breath.

That tiny moment is the perfect time to make your move. Instead of slowing at the crest, put on a sudden burst of speed as you round the top. You'll take your rival by surprise and open up a sudden gap between the two of you.

If there are significant downhill portions of the course, you need to be ready to take full advantage of these as well. Running downhill is as much a skill as running uphill. You must overcome the tendency to put the brakes on, which puts excess stress on the quads and tires them out prematurely. Instead, practice downhill running in your training, focusing on leaning forward and taking short, quick steps. If you can master this technique, you'll fly past other runners on the downhill portions and feel fresher during the final push to the finish line.

Get the Aid You Need but No More than That

Throughout Europe, most races offer aid on the course only every 5K (3.1 miles). In the United States, it's common to have an aid station at every mile. Many runners think that if water and sports drink are offered on the course, they should take it. That's simply not true.

Think of aid stations as available options; drop in for a cup when you feel thirsty. If your skin is dry or you haven't urinated all day—or worse, if your urine is darkish yellow—it's time to drink in order to avoid dehydration. Otherwise, skip a station or two and save the time and also avoid possible overhydration and hyponatremia. (Also known as water poisoning, hyponatremia is a potentially dangerous condition in which the body's electrolyte levels become diluted, which compromises muscle contractions and brain function.) Over the course of a race, skipping a few stations could mean the difference between a good finish time and a PR.

On the other hand, don't skip a necessary port-a-potty stop just to save a few moments. Feeling uncomfortable as you run will take a toll and force you to slow down. It's best in the long term to take a toilet break when you need to and then run fast and relaxed afterward.

Win the Mind Game

Over the years, I've run a great number of marathons and half-marathons. This has led some people to conclude that these races must be easy for me. I told them that, even though I run with a high degree of confidence, these were all long races and I still struggle and suffer, in my way. I just don't talk much about any suffering, having learned some tricks to keep my mind on track and keep the demons at bay.

Some of these tricks involve reminding myself about those people who have supported my running, including, first and foremost, my family. I also think about people I would like to honor with my effort and about others I wish were still with me, who would be proud to watch me cross the finish line.

I also keep a stock of short, simple phrases that help move me forward, like "You've worked hard for this" and "Just run." Many elite athletes use these kinds of phrases to maintain motivation and focus during their races. Champion marathoner Deena Kastor reportedly likes to repeat "Define yourself" during her races.

But I think we all need something more to get through the really tough moments in long-distance racing. It helps to understand, at a deep level, why you run. Understanding this makes it easier to summon the determination you need to go on when it would be so easy—and tempting—to stop. I've spent a lot of time over the years pondering this.

Take some time during your training to think about why *you* run, why you keep going when other people would stop, and why you feel compelled to try something many people wouldn't even consider. When the difficult moments occur in your races—as they surely will—remind yourself why you are there and what it took to get there. Then keep moving forward and earn the finish that you worked so hard for.

7

Avoiding Injury

AN UNDERLYING THEME THROUGHOUT THIS BOOK has been avoiding injury. Along with maximizing running potential, staying injury-free is a central goal of this training program. To this point we've focused on developing balance and strength throughout key muscle groups and developing the core. Doing this work consistently will eliminate most sources of running injuries. However, there are other things you can and should do to increase your odds of avoiding any forced layoffs.

MAINTAIN PROPER FORM

Unfortunately, you cannot control all of your body's movements while running. Some aspects of your running are beyond your control, like the way your foot hits the ground or your body's use of available fuel. Some of these things can be managed or controlled over time through training. But others, such as pronation, can't be consciously controlled and must be managed instead.

Some aspects of your running form, however, are totally within your control if you can maintain focus while running. Creating a mental checklist of these items for review while running will help you run properly and avoid the injuries that can result from running improperly. Here are some questions to include on your checklist:

Am I swinging my arms correctly? You should be swinging from the shoulder, with wrists straight and palms facing inward. Don't let your arm cross over your body as you run.

Am I engaging my abdominals? Remember to engage your transverse abdominus, as discussed in the sidebar in Chapter 2. This helps you keep your pelvis in the proper position for running and improves your overall posture.

Am I taking the right number of steps? The ideal leg turnover rate is 180 steps per minute. If you've followed this training program, you should be able to sense when you're close to hitting your goal or when you're overstriding and taking too few steps. Modify your stride as necessary as you run.

Am I relaxed? It is not uncommon to see runners with shoulders hunched high around their ears, hands balled into fists, and bodies frozen with tension. This wastes energy and strains the upper back and neck muscles.

Don't make this mistake. Push your shoulders down away from your ears to relax your shoulders, and occasionally shake your arms out to keep your upper body loose. Ease tension in your hands by imaging that you're holding a single potato chip in each hand.

Do I know what I most often do wrong while running? Keeping these in mind will help you prioritize your checklist. Personally, I know that I have a tendency to roll my shoulders instead of swing my arms, so I've spent a lot of time working on maintaining the proper arm movement while running, with good results. Having your gait analyzed will help you identify your bad habits.

PRIORITIZE REST

Most endurance athletes are very dedicated and hardworking. Many of them are type A personalities already, and they know that there are no shortcuts to a race finish line. Many of them regularly wake up before dawn to follow a grueling training schedule and are willing to suffer through discomfort and even pain. So, not surprisingly, one area where many athletes fall short is getting enough sleep.

This is a big problem. As discussed in Chapter 1, training causes micro-trauma to muscle cells, which triggers an adaptation process that resculpts the body. For this adaptation process to work, you have to give your body the downtime to make repairs. During sleep, your body releases human growth hormone, a key triggering component of the process. If you don't sleep, you don't get your full allotment of HGH and the necessary repairs and improvements are not made. Trauma layers on trauma, and your muscles become unable to fully respond to all that you ask of them. Your performance becomes compromised, and you move closer and closer to sustaining a serious injury. All for the lack of enough sleep.

HOW SAFE IS BAREFOOT RUNNING?

Barefoot running and running in minimal-support shoes have gained popularity in recent years. Proponents of minimal-support running claim that traditional running shoes weaken the muscles of the foot by relieving them of the stress needed to maintain proper muscle tone. They liken the foot to a structural arch, which relies on the tension between the stones to keep its form. If you push upward against the arch, you disrupt this tension and destabilize the structure. They also point out that our bodies evolved without shoes, so wearing shoes is unnatural and unnecessary.

Is all this true? There's some evidence that it is. But I hesitate to adopt the entire shoeless philosophy. After all, even though humans might have evolved on the soft plains of the Serengeti, most of us now live in cities and run on concrete and asphalt. And over the decades that technical running shoes have been available, they've served many runners well.

So what are we to do? I suggest incorporating some shoeless drills and barefoot running, but in moderation. Ultimately, you have to see what works best for you, but as with any new training mode, I recommend caution until you see how your body responds. For decades, running coaches have had their athletes run short intervals in the grass alongside the tracks where they were training. I recommend the same, along with a limited number of miles run weekly in minimal-support shoes.

The obvious answer is to sleep more, but for many athletes life isn't as simple as that. With work and family obligations, it's hard to get everything done while also getting in all of the scheduled workouts. Something's got to give, and usually it's sleep. To get in the standard eight hours, something else would have to be cut, and for many athletes that's not an option.

There's no easy answer to this problem. For many athletes, myself included, this is an issue that needs to be addressed daily. An important first step toward finding the proper balance between training and rest is to recognize that rest is as important as training. After all, it's during the rest and recovery phase that the gains in your training actually occur.

There will be some days when your alarm clock goes off, signaling that it's time for you to get up for your morning workout, but you'll want nothing so much as to roll over and go back to sleep. If your hesitation is nothing more than the gravitational pull of a warm bed, throw off the covers and get up. But if you're truly tired, you need to consider whether sleep would be more productive for you than a workout. Instead of pushing yourself through a subpar workout, a better plan might be to take a day off and come back stronger the next day. Not only will you be more effective in your training, but you also will reduce your risk of injury.

Keep in mind, however, that an ambitious training plan allows for only a limited number of missed workouts. If you find yourself skipping workouts on a regular basis, you'll have to reexamine your schedule and commitment to it and decide whether you can realistically return to a full training schedule. This might require more discipline than you ever imagined.

EAT WELL

Getting rest won't help your body repair itself if you haven't given it the materials necessary to make repairs. Proper nutrition is a crucial component of any effective training program. This subject deserves its own book, and indeed there are many good sports nutrition books available, such as Monique Ryan's *Sports Nutrition for Endurance Athletes*. But for our purposes here, a quick review of the role of nutrition in healing the body and avoiding injury will put us on the right track.

Proteins are often called the building blocks of the body. They provide the basic material for reconstruction of cells, including not just those within your muscles but also those making up your immune system. To stay injury-free, you need to make sure that your body has an adequate amount of protein available for use.

How much protein do you need? A good rule of thumb is that as an active athlete, you need at least a half-gram to a full gram of protein for every pound of body weight. In practice, many people are surprised that they don't hit this target. For example, if you had milk at breakfast and a chicken sandwich for lunch, you might think that you'd eaten enough protein, but given that an average fist-sized chicken breast has about 30 grams of protein and milk has about 1 gram of protein per ounce, you'd actually be only about halfway to meeting your nutritional needs.

To hit their target, then, many athletes rely on processed protein in the form of powders, shakes, or energy bars. I prefer to use these products only as last resort. I also hate to be a slave to numbers when I'm eating; I don't want to reduce my dinner to a field experiment. I've found that a concerted effort to include a good protein source at breakfast, lunch, and dinner usually meets my protein needs.

In general, the best foods are the ones that are locally sourced and processed the least because these retain the most nutrients and have the fewest preservatives. As with your choice of exercises, the best approach is to include as wide a variety of foods as possible. Protein sources should include skinless poultry, low-fat dairy, lean meat, and vegetable sources such as quinoa, beans, and legumes. If you are a vegetarian, you'll have to work a bit harder to make sure that you meet all of your nutritional needs, but this might be something that you're used to already. Being a vegetarian should not be an obstacle to attaining your racing goals, however; many elite runners are vegetarians.

If you must buy processed foods, aim to buy them in as natural a state as possible. Get in the habit of reading food labels. One basic rule is that if the list of ingredients on a label is more than four lines long, the product is no longer food; it's something else. Keep that in mind as you roam the supermarket aisles.

Many athletes ask about high-protein diets. These have been largely discredited as a healthy approach to eating because they place enormous strain on the kidneys and don't usually result in a sustainable lifestyle. As a runner, you need carbs as a primary fuel source, so even though protein plays a crucial part in your diet, it cannot be your primary nutrient. Complex carbs should still take up roughly two-thirds of your daily caloric intake.

STOCK YOUR TOOLBOX

Someone once asked me if it's possible to get too many massages. If there's a downside to frequent massage, I haven't heard about it. Short of being driven into bankruptcy, get a massage as often as possible, preferably at least every other week during hard training. Regular massage helps keep your muscles and ligaments loose and pliable, improves the flow of blood and nutrients, and helps to flush toxins and waste products.

In an ideal world, you would be able to afford a private massage therapist on a daily basis. But if that is not the case, then there's Plan B, which involves supplementing sessions you do get with some therapies you can apply yourself effectively and cheaply at home. Here are the tools you'll need and a brief description of how to employ them.

Foam roller. Formerly available only at the physical therapist's office, this hard foam cylinder is used to self-massage various body parts (Fig. 7.1). Lay it on the floor, and roll your target body part back and forth over it slowly, spending extra time on any area that feels sore.

The foam roller is especially useful for working on the IT band. Lie on your side and place the roller crosswise under your hip. Then push your body on the roller for the length of your upper leg until the roller is near the outside of your knee.

There isn't much muscle or fat on the outside of your leg, so the roller will be pressing your IT band right into your thighbone. I won't lie to you; that's going to be painful. But if it doesn't hurt a bit, you're not doing it right. Using the roller this way will never feel good, but eventually it will feel a bit less terrible. As you get used to it, try to

7.1

balance all your weight on the roller instead of just dragging your body along—that will give you a deeper and
more effective massage of that area.

Massage stick. This is another useful tool for self-
massage. Think of it as a rolling pin and your body as a
big lump of dough, and then get to work (Fig. 7.2). Try
to hold your body so that the muscle you are working
on is soft and loose, which will make the massage more
effective.

The massage stick can easily work your legs and with a
little practice (and perhaps help from a partner) can work
your back as well. The hamstrings are an area especially
well suited for attention from the massage stick. Sit down
and bend your knee at a 90-degree angle, with your foot
flat on the floor and your hamstring hanging loose. Place
the massage stick under your leg and across your muscle,
and roll it back and forth along the length of the muscle,

7.2

pulling on the stick as hard as you comfortably can. Hamstrings are a frequently injured muscle group and slow to heal, but they respond well to
this treatment.

Wobble board. This apparatus is simply a disc, usually made of wood,
with a hard rubber half-sphere attached to the middle of its underside (Fig.
7.3). This creates an unstable surface to stand on, making it useful for improving balance. Our goal, however, is to use it to increase the range of motion in your tight runner's ankles.

Stand with one foot placed in the center of the wobble board and the other
foot held off to the side. Place a
hand on a wall or chair back for
support if necessary. Now shift
your weight around on the board,
causing it to touch the ground
around it in a circular pattern.
Do 10 clockwise rotations and 10
counterclockwise rotations; then
switch to the other foot.

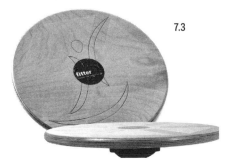

7.3

THE TRUTH ABOUT STRETCHING

How important is stretching for a runner? That's harder to answer than you might think.

To date, there is no evidence that stretching improves running performance. In fact, to the contrary, research indicates that stretching can actually weaken you (Fowles, Sale, and MacDougall 2000). This makes sense when you consider the way the body functions: Our bones are really just levers connected by ligaments and powered by muscles. Your body operates under tension; without tension, your body would hardly be able to remain upright, let alone run.

This conception of the body is reflected in a work of art at the Smithsonian National Gallery of Art in Washington, DC, called Pinz Friedrich von Homburg, ein Schauspiel, 3X. Made of aluminum, stainless steel, fiberglass, and carbon fiber, the sculpture weighs just shy of 10 tons and looks a lot like a car wreck. The genius of the piece, however, is that each of its elements both supports and pulls against other elements, resulting in a balance of tension that allows the piece to stand upright. A reduction in tension would cause the sculpture to collapse.

This is essentially how our bodies work.

I'm not against stretching, however. Stretching helps relieve the symptoms of specific injuries and helps prevent the onset of others. It also just feels good. And even if we can't prove that stretching helps, most researchers and coaches believe that it probably does some good, if only to help increase and maintain range of motion and improve blood flow.

But when you are faced with an injury that is a result of tightness or may be alleviated by increased flexibility in the affected areas, it is key not just to perform recommended stretches but also to ask what caused the tightness in the first place. Without addressing the underlying problem, the injury may be managed but not resolved.

8

Beyond the Marathon

AFTER YOU'VE WORKED SO HARD to summit a distant peak and achieved that goal, an unexpected problem may arise: What do you do once you've gotten to the top? One answer, of course, is that you continue to climb that mountain again and again, learning more of its secrets—and your own—with each ascent, much like scholars have mined Shakespeare's works for centuries in search of new insights. Or sometimes you just look for other mountains to climb.

After you've run your target race and achieved your goal, you'll have plenty of options for new challenges to take on. You could aim to improve your time even more or to take on the same race distance in another city on another course. Another option is to take on a different kind of endurance challenge altogether. With your hard-earned conditioning and balanced strength, there are a great many possibilities waiting out there for you. Some are described here.

THE ULTRAMARATHON

For experienced runners, the challenge of racing lies in perfecting training plans and improving finishing times. There may be nerves before the start of the race, but there is usually little question about being able to cross the finish line. The question is whether they will do it quickly or slowly.

It hasn't always been that way, of course. For all of us, there was a first long-distance race. And before that, there was a longest-ever training run. Before we conquered those distances, most of us had moments of fear or concern that we might not be up to the challenge. In my coaching, I've seen some new marathoners who doubted they could run 26.2 miles at all, even as they were approaching the finish line. When a finisher's medal was finally draped around their necks, the emotion of having achieved a dream was often overwhelming.

That moment—that mixture of relief and joy—can never quite be replicated. In future races, those athletes already *know* that they are capable of finishing; their concern will center more on what their finishing times will be or what quirks a particular course presents. But they will never again experience quite that same unique mix of fear and excitement that happened the first time they ran a long-distance race.

Unless, that is, they move up to a longer distance. For half-marathoners, the marathon looms. For marathoners, there's the ultramarathon.

An *ultramarathon* is defined as any race distance that's longer than 26.2 miles. Many races fall within this category, including 100K and 24-hour races. Traditionally, however, most ultramarathons fall into three distances: the 50K, the 50-miler, and the 100-miler.

When we look at those numbers, it's sometimes hard to imagine being able to actually run such long distances. But many people do—people who have no special skills or gifts. And if you're interested, you could do it, too. Really.

Here's why: If you've worked your way up to the marathon, you've already taught your body the most essential skill of long-distance running, which is burning fat as fuel. As discussed in Chapter 2, your body's preferred fuel for movement is glycogen. Fat is a much more plentiful energy source, but your body won't start using fat unless it has to. By the time you've acclimated to long runs of 2 hours or more, your body has made that transition.

From that point on, running an ultra is just a matter of asking your body to do more of the same. That's why I tell the athletes I coach that it's actually harder to shift from a 5K or 10K to a marathon than it is to go from a marathon to a 50-miler.

In another sense, however, the ultra is unlike almost any other race you can do because most of them are run on trails, not roads. There's something about running in the woods that changes the way you look at time and distance. Without street signs and mile markers flashing by, it's easier to lose yourself in the woods and settle into a calm rhythm. At the same time, variations on the trail, such as rocks and tree roots, demand your attention. This engages you mentally and helps take your mind off the discomforts or doubts you might be experiencing.

At this point, you might still think that running an ultra is crazy, and I wouldn't disagree. As the joke goes, any idiot can run a marathon, but it takes a special kind of idiot to run an ultramarathon. But before you ran a half-marathon or marathon, you probably doubted the sanity of pushing yourself to those distances. Suspend your disbelief for a few minutes more, and let's talk about how you can actually do this.

Preparing for the Ultra

As we talked about earlier in this book, the overload principle dictates that pushing the body beyond its comfort zone triggers an adaptation response that leads to increased fitness. For target races up to the half-marathon distance, this usually involves long runs during training that exceed the target race distance. But as discussed earlier, this does not apply to the marathon because the risk of injury from running so far outweighs the benefits of the workout.

This shift away from overloading the body during training is even more pronounced when you prepare for the ultramarathon. As you can see in Table 8.1, the longer the target race distance is, the smaller is the percentage of that distance you need to cover in training.

Still, when training for an ultramarathon, you need to do a long run of 35 miles or more. This raises an interesting possibility for your ultramarathon training. You might find it more fun to do your long run among thousands of other runners on a fully supported course, instead of doing it on your own. In other words, you could use a marathon as a training run for an ultra.

TABLE 8.1		
TRAINING DISTANCES FOR TARGET RACES		
TARGET RACE	LONGEST TRAINING RUN (MILES)	LONGEST TRAINING RUN AT % OF TARGET RACE
5K	10	300
10K	12	200
HALF-MARATHON	14 – 16	110 – 120
MARATHON	20 – 22	75 – 80
50-MILER	35	70
100-MILER	60 – 65	60 – 65

Just run the course at your planned training pace—which will be 60 to 90 seconds slower than your marathon race pace—and then continue running after crossing the finish line until you get in all of your scheduled miles.

There's one caveat with this plan: If you end up treating the marathon as a real race instead of a training run, you might put too much wear and tear on your body to continue with your training for the ultra. As a rule of thumb, plan on needing a day off or an easy day of training for every hard mile you race, so if you race a marathon instead of using it as a planned training run, you might need up to 4 weeks to recover from your effort.

That's too long a break from your ultramarathon preparation. So to do this right, you must be disciplined. You can't let yourself get caught up in the race-day excitement. Starting near the back of the pack helps because you won't have as many people passing you as the race develops. This eliminates some of the temptation to speed up.

Apart from building your endurance base, there are a few other things to consider in your ultra training. Given that the conditions in the ultra will be significantly different from what you're used to in more traditional races, you need to try to simulate some of those conditions in your training. Your target ultra will probably be on trails, which is their most common course, so you'll need to get used to trail running. If there are lots of changes in elevation, you'll also need to add more hill work. And if there are very technical sections on the course, such as crossing a stream or traversing loose rock, you should practice doing that as well.

For the 100-miler, you can count on having to run at least 24 hours, which means you will have to run straight through the night from sunset to sunrise, all while feeling very fatigued. There's no way to fully simulate in training what this feels like, but if you're planning on doing a 100-miler, you need to at least run through the night once in training.

You also need to pay even closer attention to race-day nutrition when racing an ultra. A good marathon race plan includes taking in some easily digested nutrition every hour, such as an energy gel. In an ultra, however, you would plan to be on the course for at least twice as long as you would in a road race, so your body's nutritional needs are greater. A gel simply won't cut it when you're starting to feel hungry 5 or 6 hours into your race. Solid food is a must, but you need to get your body acclimated to digesting solid food while running.

Don't wait for race day to sort this out. Find out what will be offered on the racecourse, and try these foods during training to see what works best for you. Typical aid station fare includes peanut butter and jelly sandwiches, cookies and fig bars, baked potatoes (which provides potassium along with carbs), and chicken noodle soup.

Here's the best ultramarathoning advice you'll ever get: *Be patient.* It sounds simple, but it's harder to execute than you might think. On race day, once you've got a few hours of running under your belt and feel warmed up, you'll find yourself settling into a comfortable race pace, just as in regular road races. It will feel easy, so you won't sense any danger, but danger is there nonetheless. You are going too fast. A pace that feels comfortable for a few hours of running is going to be hard to maintain for 7 hours or more, and somewhere down the trail, you're going to slow to a walk, then maybe a crawl. This is where the DNF ("did not finish") is born. On the other hand, if you can keep to an excruciatingly easy pace and maintain it for the entire race, you'll end up with a great day.

One way to stay on track is to walk the steep uphills, especially when you see other runners doing that. In my first 50-miler, I could tell from all the conversations going on around me that there was a lot of cumulative

ULTRAMARATHONING TIPS

Accept that it takes a small village to run an ultra. Most runners are fiercely independent, but as the target distance gets longer and longer, dependence on support teams becomes more and more necessary. This is especially true if you plan to run a 100-miler. For that distance, most racers assemble their own support team to shadow them on the course, providing food, drink, medical aid, encouragement, and camaraderie.

Make sure you choose your support team carefully, however. Team members are there for a specific task: to give you the best possible chance of reaching the finish line. If you have a family member or friend who would like to be part of the team but who lacks necessary skills or group compatibility, don't invite him. The last thing you'll want to deal with in the middle of the night after running for 12 hours is squabbling and bickering in your support team.

Once you assemble your team, show team members your appreciation. After all, they've just signed up to dedicate a chunk of their time to do everything they can to help you pursue your dream. That's a pretty special gift.

Be a camel. Take your own hydration pack. Aid stations are much farther apart in an ultra—often 6 miles or more—and you can get very dehydrated when running for hours, especially if it is a warm day.

Don't linger in the aid stations. It's tempting to do so because you'll be tired and there will be plenty of food and drink, along with people to chat with. But don't hang around. Aid stations can be a subtle time killer. If you spend 10 or 15 minutes at each, which isn't hard to do, you'll have added an hour or more to your finishing time. Plus, after every delay it becomes harder physically and emotionally to get yourself moving again. So grab what you need and go.

Use only gear you trust. The longer the race is, the more that small issues have a chance to become big issues. Everything you use in an ultra, from clothing to food to sunglasses, should be as familiar to you as the back of your hand. If you have any issues with anything in your kit, change it.

While we're on this subject, here's a word about shoes: You don't need to run out to buy trail shoes. Even though some people prefer using those, many successful ultrarunners use regular road shoes. Focus instead on simply using shoes that are appropriate for you and are comfortable.

Know your course. In a road race, a hill might just be a rise in the road and a big hill might be an incline. But on a trail, which is where most ultras are held, a hill might be a massive, rocky climb. I once signed up for a 50-miler without checking on details about the course, only to discover on race day that it was considered one of the most difficult ultras in the United States. Do your homework so that on race day you are challenged but not overwhelmed.

ultrarunning experience among these runners. So when I saw them all walking the hills, I figured that must be the right thing to do. And it was. By following their lead, I saved some energy for the last miles, when I needed it the most.

There's a lot more to say about ultrarunning—this is only an introduction. But like running itself, you might find that once you try an ultra, you'll be hooked for life.

THE TRIATHLON

If an ultra sounds a bit too crazy for you, then a triathlon might make better sense to you. After all, with all of the cycling and running you've been doing in this program, you're already a multisport athlete.

When people think of the triathlon, many automatically think that means an Ironman race, which consists of a 2.25-mile swim, a 112-mile ride, and a 26.2-mile run. But that's not the only—or even the most popular—triathlon race distance. A sprint triathlon varies in distance, but commonly consists of an 800-meter swim, a 20K ride, and a 5K run. The sprint can be completed in 2 hours or less. The international distance, or, as it is sometimes called, the Olympic distance, is more settled, consisting of a 1,500-meter swim, a 40K ride, and a 10K run. Most athletes complete this course in 2–3 hours. With the endurance base you've developed in your road race training, you're already well positioned to complete either race.

So what's holding you back? If you're like many runners, you're probably concerned about the swim. That makes sense. Runners condition their neuromuscular systems to move their bodies in certain ways. Also, the repeated stress on their tendons and ligaments from running has probably reduced their flexibility, especially in the ankles. So instead of sliding gracefully through the water like fish, with their feet extended, most runners flap around in the water, dragging their feet behind them like anchors.

I struggle with this myself. I was once told that I swim like a runner, which was not meant as a compliment. Another friend, who happens to be a competitive master swimmer, told me that what I do in the water looks less like swimming and more like very slow drowning.

But I'm working on it, and I'm slowly getting better. And so can you.

Preparing for a Triathlon

The first thing that you need to do if you're not a good swimmer is to understand that you don't need to be a *great* swimmer to be a good triathlete. You really just need to be good enough to make it through the swim leg. After that, you can make up time on the cycle and running legs of the race, which are areas in which you already excel.

Once you've mastered the basics of swimming, you could spend time improving your swim time. But with the swim leg shorter in time and distance than the cycle and running legs, you could perhaps more easily improve your overall race times if you spent those same hours working on cycling and running instead, where big increases in speed are more common.

Still, doing triathlon is more than just swimming, cycling, and running. It's combining all those things to form something new, something bigger than the sum of its parts. That's trickier than you might first think. Triathletes often refer to this as the challenge of making order out of chaos. As always, you should aim to sort out these issues in training before you line up on race day.

The biggest change in your training routine will be the introduction of the brick workout. A *brick* is composed of two or more elements of a triathlon performed back-to-back in training. The goal is to acclimatize the body to the rigors of reaching fatigue in one mode while retaining the ability to continue on in another mode, all without stopping.

The origin of this term most likely comes from the way your legs feel when you try running after having gotten off the bike. All triathletes experience this dead-leg feeling; you'll just need to grin and bear it, knowing that after a mile or two, your legs will settle into a groove.

Triathlon is one of the fastest-growing sports in the country, and there are a lot of resources that have been developed to help newbie triathletes. Seminars, training programs, and books such as Joe Friel's *The Triathlete's Training Bible* offer excellent advice for getting you started on the right track. Check if there is a triathlon club in your area. That's a good place to find information about participation opportunities in your area. In addition, the USA Triathlon web site has great resources on everything from training to racing to finding information about events in your area. Check out www.USATriathlon.org.

UNCONVENTIONAL RACING

OBSTACLE-COURSE OR MUD RACING

This racing format has steadily been gaining in popularity. Whether set up as a slog through a muddy trail course with a teammate or as a full obstacle course involving hurdling high walls, crawling under wire, carrying logs, and running through fire, these races offer a fun, challenging alternative to regular road racing.

These races favor participants who are not only fast but who also have developed good core and upper body strength. After completing my program, you're absolutely ready to take a dive into a race like this.

These are timed races, but because each course is unique, the finishing times are relevant only to the competitors participating in that race on that day. No one talks about PRs; the goal is simply to finish the race, and the standout participants are those who are barely visible underneath the mud and dirt they've collected on themselves.

PUMP-N-RUN RACE

A lesser-known racing opportunity, but one that you would be well suited to after using the Smart Marathon Training program, is a pump-n-run race. This race isn't offered everywhere, so do a Web search to find the one nearest to you. But if you can find one, you'll be happy that you made the effort. This race aims to test your balance of strength and speed and is usually framed as a competition within an existing road race.

Pump-n-run competitions usually work like this: Just before the race begins, participants are weighed. A barbell on a bench press station situated nearby is then loaded up—usually at two-thirds of the measured body weight for women and the full body weight for men, although sometimes the amounts are age-adjusted instead. Then the participant lifts away, aiming to do as many chest presses with the weight as he or she can.

Totals are noted, and then all participants line up for the race. Afterward, 1 minute is deducted from their finishing time for each repetition they completed earlier. The lowest net scores receive prizes.

This is a racing format that I especially like because it suits me so well. I may not be a very fast runner, but I'm pretty fast for a weight lifter. And even though I may not be a very powerful weight lifter, I'm pretty strong for a runner. With a pump-n-run, I finally have a shot at winning some awards. Best of all, it's fun.

WHAT ABOUT FUN?

If you've read this far, your mind is probably clicking away like a high-speed computer, figuring out how to mesh together all of the elements of your training routine in order to produce the best possible race results. The purpose of this book has been to give you the tools to make those decisions.

But while you're writing down your season training and racing plan, you might find yourself longing for the days when you could go for an easy run, with no concern about speed or split times or pacing or how the run fits into your training schedule. You might find yourself asking, what happened to running for the fun of it?

I'm glad you asked. Very few people can race near their potential for very long. Although there's great personal satisfaction in realizing your road racing dreams, working at that level can be physically and mentally exhausting. Taking a break from focused running is a crucial element in any training plan. After competing in your target race, take a break. It might be only for a week or two, or it might be for several months, but at some point every year forget about your training plan. Run for fun, the way you probably did before you ever crossed a finish line.

Finding it difficult to let go? Here are some tricks:

Run without a watch. The late, great running philosopher and cardiologist Dr. George Sheehan once wrote about the stages of running, concluding that the ultimate stage was when you could leave your watch at home and run for as far as you felt like it and whatever pace you felt like running. Take Dr. Sheehan's description as literal advice in order to avoid race burnout.

Run a new route. One way to avoid calculating your splits during training is to run on an unfamiliar route where you're not aware of the mileage. Without having a history of running that route, you'll have no ghosts of runs past to compete against. If this sounds complicated, then simply run your same old route in reverse. You'll be amazed at how different it will seem.

Run to a location. Explore something on your route that forces you to slow down or stop. Historic markers are a good example. During hard training, I never allow myself the luxury of reading these, although I know that the information contained on them would make the runs that much more meaningful for me. So I use my downtime to catch up on this bit of sightseeing. Look for any opportunity to literally stop and smell the roses.

Run for the company. Invite a slower, less-competitive friend or two to join you for a social run. It's a nice way to catch up with folks, and you'll feel refreshed by the joy of moving while having a conversation. Top it off with a post-run coffee/tea/snack stop.

9

Training
Schedules

UP TO THIS POINT, we've spent our time reviewing the theory and details of what a balanced running program should contain. Now it's time to get out your calendar or training log and actually map out your own personal program.

Listed in this chapter are six detailed training schedules, each of which incorporates all of the training concepts we've reviewed in this book. Three are for the half-marathon, and three are for the marathon. These schedules are further divided into intermediate, advanced, and competitive categories. The *intermediate* programs are targeted at runners who have a solid base and who may or may not have competed in that distance already, have not competed at that distance in more than a year, or are returning to that distance following an injury-induced layoff. The *advanced* programs are for runners who have raced that distance several times already. The *competitive* programs are for more experienced runners who are looking to better their PR or, having experienced a layoff owing to injury, want to safely get back to where they were.

These programs might be a little different from others that you've read because you cannot simply follow any of these blindly, even if you wanted to. You will need to make choices, especially concerning the core and strength workouts. By now, having read all the preceding materials, you should be familiar with what your choices are. Still, when you draw up a training schedule, it's easy to get lost in the details and to forget the main points of the program. Here are some guidelines to keep in mind.

- *Avoid repeating.* Keep the workouts fresh and effective by changing your routine so that you never do the same strength or core workout twice in a row.
- *Don't worry about how much time it takes.* Schedule 30–40 minutes for your strength routine for your first few weeks. Over time, you'll become more comfortable with the exercises and more proficient in doing them, so you should be able to get through that same workout in just 20–30 minutes.
- *Resist the urge to be an overachiever.* Do not spend more time doing strength training than you've scheduled. Exercise tends to follow the Newtonian rule on equal and opposite reactions: The more intense and lengthy the effort you put in early on, the more likely you'll be to burn out and avoid strength training altogether down the road. Sometimes it's my job to protect people from their own enthusiasm. As I tell my clients, be smarter than you are brave—do all the work you have to do, but then walk away.
- *There is no single perfect schedule; there is only the routine that works best for you.* On some days, you will be going through multiple workouts, such as strength training, core training, and cycling. Each workout is important, but the order and timing of the workouts are up to you. Some people like to start with cardio work to warm up thoroughly and then get right into strength training afterward, whereas others feel more comfortable doing the reverse. Still others split these workouts up and spread them across the day. All of these options are valid; the final decision depends on what you prefer.

In the schedules that follow, you'll also find references to the cycling crosstraining workouts. As we discussed in Chapter 3, you should be sure to include some hill climbs at least once per week to build power and speed. You should also practice your cycling drills at least once per week.

The speed work workouts included in the schedule charts refer to those listed by number directly following each chart.

INTERMEDIATE HALF-MARATHON

WEEK	SUN LRR	MON STR/CORE*	TUE X-TR	WED SPD/HW	THUR STR/CORE/X-TR	FRI TR	SAT OFF
1	8	Cable, Core Ride 15 mi.	Off	HW x 4 Drills	MCH, Core	7	Off
2	10	FWT, Core Ride 20 mi.	Off	HW x 6 Drills	BWT, Core Ride 10 mi. (fast)	7	Off
3	12	Cable, Core Ride 25 mi.	Off	SPD #1 Drills	MCH, Core Ride 15 mi. (fast)	8	Off
4	6	FWT, Core Ride 30 mi.	Off	SPD #2 Drills	BWT, Core Ride 15 mi. (fast)	8	Off
5	10	FWT, Core Ride 35 mi.	Off	SPD #3 Drills	BWT, Core Ride 15 mi. (fast)	8	Off
6	14	Cable, Core Ride 40 mi.	Off	SPD #4 Drills	MCH, Core Ride 20 mi.	8	Off
7	Ride 20 mi.	TR 6	SPD #5	Off	Core (short)	Drills	Off
8	HALF-MARATHON						

SPEED WORKOUTS

1-MILE WARM-UP, INTERVALS, 1-MILE COOLDOWN

1. 8 × 400 m
   with 200 m recoveries
   (5K race pace)

2. 400 m, 800 m, 400 m
   with 400 m recoveries
   (10K race pace)
   Repeat 3 times

3. 400 m, 800 m, 1,200 m,
   800 m, 400 m

   with 400 m recoveries
   (10K race pace)
   Repeat 3 times

4. 6 × 800 m
   with 400 m recoveries
   (10K race pace)

5. 4 × 200 m
   with 200 m recoveries
   (5K race pace)

KEY

LRR = Long Run or Ride   STR = Strength Training   CORE = Core Training   X-TR = Crosstraining
SPD = Speed Workout   HW = Hill Workout   TR = Tempo Run

MCH = Machine Workout   FWT = Free-Weight Workout   BWT = Body-Weight Workout
Combo = includes FWT, BWT, MCH, and Cable in the same workout

Note: *Run workouts are in bold. mi. = miles*

*At least one of your core workouts every week should include functional strength work, found in Ch. 4.

++ ADVANCED HALF-MARATHON

WEEK	SUN LRR	MON STR/CORE*	TUE X-TR	WED SPD/HW	THUR STR/CORE/X-TR	FRI TR	SAT OFF
1	8	Cable, Core	Ride 20 mi.	HW x 4 Drills	MCH, Core Ride 20 mi. (fast)	7	Off
2	10	FWT, Core	Ride 25 mi.	HW x 6 Drills	BWT, Core Ride 20 mi. (fast)	7	Off
3	12	Cable, Core	Ride 25 mi. (hilly)	HW x 6 Drills	MCH, Core Ride 25 mi. (fast)	8	Off
4	8	FWT, Core	Ride 25 mi. (hilly)	HW x 8 Drills	BWT, Core Ride 25 mi. (fast)	8	Off
5	14	Cable, Core	Ride 25 mi.	HW x 8 Drills	MCH, Core Ride 20 mi. (fast)	8	Off
6	8	FWT, Core	Ride 30 mi.	SPD #1 Drills	BWT, Core Ride 25 mi. (fast)	8	Off
7	16	Cable, Core	Ride 35 mi.	SPD #2 Drills	MCH, Core Ride 25 mi. (fast)	8	Off
8	Ride 40 mi.	Combo, Core	TR 10	SPD #3 Drills	FWT, Core Ride 25 mi. (fast)	8	Off
9	16	Cable, Core	Ride 30 mi. hilly	SPD #4 Drills	MCH, Core Ride 25 mi. (fast)	8	Off
10	Ride 50 mi.	FWT, Core	TR 8	SPD #5 Drills	BWT, Core Ride 20 mi. (fast)	8	Off
11	TR 6	Cable, Core	SPD #6	Core	Ride 10 mi.	Drills	Off
12	HALF-MARATHON						

SPEED WORKOUTS
1-MILE WARM-UP, INTERVALS, 1-MILE COOLDOWN

1. 10×400 m
   with 200 m recoveries
   (5K race pace)

2. 400 m, 1,200 m, 400 m
   with 400 m recoveries
   (10K race pace)
   Repeat 3 times

3. 12×400 m
   with 200 m recoveries
   (5K race pace)

4. 8×800 m
   with 400 m recoveries
   (10K race pace)

5. 400 m, $2 \times 1,600$ m, 400 m
   with 400 m recoveries
   (10K race pace)

6. 4×200 m
   with 200 m recoveries
   (5K race pace)

KEY

LRR = Long Run or Ride **STR** = Strength Training **CORE** = Core Training **X-TR** = Crosstraining
SPD = Speed Workout **HW** = Hill Workout **TR** = Tempo Run

MCH = Machine Workout **FWT** = Free-Weight Workout **BWT** = Body-Weight Workout
Combo = includes FWT, BWT, MCH, and Cable in the same workout

Note: *Run workouts are in bold. mi. = miles*

*At least one of your core workouts every week should include functional strength work, found in Ch. 4.

+++ COMPETITIVE HALF-MARATHON

WEEK	SUN LRR	MON STR/CORE*	TUE X-TR	WED SPD/HW	THUR STR/CORE/X-TR	FRI TR	SAT OFF
1	10	Cable, Core	Ride 25 mi.	HW x 4 Drills	MCH, Core Ride 15 mi. (fast)	7	Off
2	10	FWT, Core	Ride 30 mi.	HW x 6 Drills	BWT, Core Ride 20 mi. (fast)	7	Off
3	12	Cable, Core	Ride 20 mi. (hilly)	HW x 6 Drills	MCH, Core Ride 20 mi. (fast)	8	Off
4	8	FWT, Core	Ride 35 mi.	HW x 8 Drills	BWT, Core Ride 25 mi. (fast)	8	Off
5	14	Cable, Core	Ride 25 mi. (hilly)	HW x 8 Drills	MCH, Core Ride 25 mi. (fast)	8	Off
6	10	FWT, Core	Ride 30 mi. (hilly)	SPD #1 Drills	BWT, Core Ride 30 mi. (fast)	8	Off
7	16	Cable, Core	Ride 30 mi. (hilly)	SPD #2 Drills	MCH, Core Ride 30 mi. (fast)	8	Off
8	Ride 40 mi.	Combo, Core	TR 10	SPD #3 Drills	FWT, Core Ride 30 mi. (fast)	8	Off
9	18	Cable, Core	Ride 30 mi. (hilly)	SPD #4 Drills	MCH, Core Ride 30 mi. (fast)	8	Off
10	Ride 60 mi.	FWT, Core	TR 8	SPD #5 Drills	BWT, Core Ride 30 mi. (fast)	8	Off
11	10	Cable, Core	Ride 30 mi. (hilly)	SPD #6 Drills	MCH, Core Ride 30 mi. (fast)	8	Off
12	18	FWT, Core	Ride 30 mi. (hilly)	SPD #7 Drills	BWT, Core Ride 30 mi. (fast)	10	Off
13	10	Cable, Core	Ride 30 mi.	SPD #8 Drills	MCH, Core Ride 30 mi. (fast)	8	Off
14	TR 6	Combo, Core	Ride 20 mi.	Core Drills	SPD #9	2	Off
15	H A L F — M A R A T H O N						

SPEED WORKOUTS

1-MILE WARM-UP, INTERVALS, 1-MILE COOLDOWN

1. 10 × 400 m
   with 200 m recoveries
   (5K race pace)

2. 400 m, 800 m, 400 m
   with 400 m recoveries
   (10K race pace)
   Repeat 3 times

3. 12 × 400 m
   with 200 m recoveries
   (5K race pace)

4. 400 m, 800 m, 1,200 m,
   800 m, 400 m
   with 400 m recoveries
   (10K race pace)
   Repeat 3 times

5. 6 × 800 m
   with 400 m recoveries
   (10K race pace)

6. 4 × 1,600 m
   with 400 m recoveries
   (10K race pace)

7. 8 × 800 m, 400 m
   with 400 m recoveries
   (10K race pace)

8. 5 × 1,600 m
   with 400 m recoveries
   (10K race pace)

9. 4 × 200 m
   with 200 m recoveries
   (5K race pace)

KEY

LRR = Long Run or Ride **STR** = Strength Training **CORE** = Core Training **X-TR** = Crosstraining
SPD = Speed Workout **HW** = Hill Workout **TR** = Tempo Run

MCH = Machine Workout **FWT** = Free-Weight Workout **BWT** = Body-Weight Workout
Combo = includes FWT, BWT, MCH, and Cable in the same workout

Note: *Run workouts are in bold. mi. = miles*

*At least one of your core workouts every week should include functional strength work, found in Ch. 4.

TRAINING SCHEDULE

+ INTERMEDIATE MARATHON

WEEK	SUN LRR	MON STR/CORE*	TUE X-TR	WED SPD/HW	THUR STR/CORE/X-TR	FRI TR	SAT OFF
1	8	Cable, Core	Ride 15 mi.	HW x 4 Drills	MCH, Core Ride 10 mi. (fast)	7	Off
2	10	FWT, Core	Ride 15 mi.	HW x 6 Drills	BWT, Core Ride 10 mi. (fast)	7	Off
3	12	Cable, Core	Ride 20 mi.	HW x 6 Drills	MCH, Core Ride 10 mi. (fast)	8	Off
4	14	FWT, Core	Ride 20 mi.	HW x 8 Drills	BWT, Core Ride 15 mi. (fast)	8	Off
5	10	Cable, Core	Ride 20 mi. (hilly)	HW x 8 Drills	MCH, Core Ride 15 mi. (fast)	8	Off
6	16	FWT, Core	Ride 20 mi. (hilly)	SPD #1 Drills	BWT, Core Ride 20 mi. (fast)	8	Off
7	10	Cable, Core	Ride 20 mi. (hilly)	SPD #2 Drills	MCH, Core Ride 20 mi. (fast)	8	Off
8	Ride 50 mi.	Combo, Core	TR 10	SPD #3 Drills	FWT, Core Ride 20 mi. (fast)	8	Off
9	18	Cable, Core	Ride 25 mi.	SPD #4 Drills	MCH, Core Ride 20 mi. (fast)	8	Off
10	Ride 60 mi.	FWT, Core	TR 8	SPD #5 Drills	BWT, Core Ride 20 mi. (fast)	8	Off
11	20	Cable, Core	Ride 25 mi.	SPD #6 Drills	MCH, Core Ride 20 mi. (fast)	8	Off
12	10	FWT, Core	Ride 20 mi. (hilly)	SPD #7 Drills	BWT, Core Ride 20 mi. (fast)	10	Off
13	14	Cable, Core	Ride 25 mi.	SPD #8 Drills	MCH, Core Ride 20 mi. (fast)	8	Off
14	Ride 60 mi.	Combo, Core	TR 8	SPD #9 Drills	FWT, Core Ride 20 mi. (fast)	8	Off
15	20	BWT, Core	Ride 20 mi. (hilly)	SPD #10 Drills	Cable, Core Ride 20 mi. (fast)	8	Off
16	10	FWT, Core	Ride 30 mi.	SPD #11 Drills	MCH, Core Ride 20 mi. (fast)	8	Off
17	Ride 60 mi.	BWT, Core	TR 8	SPD #12 Drills	FWT, Core Ride 20 mi.	8	Off
18	20	Cable, Core	Ride 20 mi. (hilly)	SPD #13 Drills	MCH, Core Ride 20 mi. (fast)	8	Off
19	10	Combo, Core	Ride 20 mi.	SPD #14 Drills	Core	Ride 15 mi.	Off
20	TR 6	Ride 15 mi. Core	Off	SPD #15	Off	Drills	Off
21	MARATHON						

SPEED WORKOUTS

1-MILE WARM-UP, INTERVALS, 1-MILE COOLDOWN

1. 8 × 400 m
   with 200 m recoveries
   (5K race pace)

2. 400 m, 800 m, 400 m
   with 400 m recoveries
   (10K race pace)
   Repeat 3 times

3. 10 × 400 m
   with 200 m recoveries
   (5K race pace)

4. 400 m, 800 m, 1,200 m,
   800 m, 400 m
   with 400 m recoveries
   (10K race pace)
   Repeat 3 times

5. 6 × 800 m
   with 400 m recoveries
   (10K race pace)

6. 3 × 1,600 m
   with 400 m recoveries
   (10K race pace)

7. 6 × 800 m, 400 m
   with 400 m recoveries
   (10K race pace)

8. 5 × 1,600 m
   with 400 m recoveries
   (10K race pace)

9. 6 × 800 m
   with 400 m recoveries and a 5-
   minute rest after repeat number 5
   (10K race pace)

10. 3 × 1,600 m
    with 400 m recoveries
    (10K race pace)

11. 20 × 400 m
    with 200 m recoveries
    (5K race pace)

12. 400 m, 800 m, 1,200 m,
    800 m, 400 m
    with 400 m recoveries
    (10K race pace)
    Repeat 3 times

13. 3 × 1,600 m
    with 400 m recoveries
    (10K race pace)

14. 400 m, 800 m, 400 m, 800 m,
    400 m, 800 m, 400 m, 800 m,
    400 m
    with 400 m recoveries
    (10K race pace)
    Repeat 2 times

15. 4 × 200 m
    with 200 m recoveries
    (5K race pace)

KEY

LRR = Long Run or Ride **STR** = Strength Training **CORE** = Core Training **X-TR** = Crosstraining
SPD = Speed Workout **HW** = Hill Workout **TR** = Tempo Run

MCH = Machine Workout **FWT** = Free-Weight Workout **BWT** = Body-Weight Workout
Combo = includes FWT, BWT, MCH, and Cable in the same workout

Note: *Run workouts are in bold. mi. = miles*

*At least one of your core workouts every week should include functional strength work, found in Ch. 4.

TRAINING SCHEDULE

++ ADVANCED MARATHON

WEEK	SUN LRR	MON STR/CORE*	TUE X-TR	WED SPD/HW	THUR STR/CORE/X-TR	FRI TR	SAT OFF
1	10	Cable, Core	Ride 20 mi.	HW x 4 Drills	MCH, Core Ride 15 mi. (fast)	7	Off
2	12	FWT, Core	Ride 15 mi. (hilly)	HW x 6 Drills	BWT, Core Ride 15 mi. (fast)	7	Off
3	14	Cable, Core	Ride 20 mi.	HW x 6 Drills	MCH, Core Ride 15 mi. (fast)	8	Off
4	6	FWT, Core	Ride 20 mi. (hilly)	HW x 8 Drills	BWT, Core Ride 15 mi. (fast)	8	Off
5	14	Cable, Core	Ride 25 mi.	HW x 8 Drills	MCH, Core Ride 15 mi. (fast)	8	Off
6	16	FWT, Core	Ride 20 mi. (hilly)	SPD #1 Drills	BWT, Core Ride 20 mi. (fast)	8	Off
7	18	Cable, Core	Ride 25 mi.	SPD #2 Drills	MCH, Core Ride 20 mi. (fast)	8	Off
8	Ride 40 mi.	Combo, Core	TR 10	SPD #3 Drills	FWT, Core Ride 20 mi. (fast)	8	Off
9	16	Cable, Core	Ride 25 mi.	SPD #4 Drills	MCH, Core Ride 20 mi. (fast)	8	Off
10	Ride 50 mi.	FWT, Core	TR 8	SPD #5 Drills	BWT, Core Ride 20 mi. (fast)	8	Off
11	20	Cable, Core	Ride 25 mi.	SPD #6 Drills	MCH, Core Ride 20 mi. (fast)	8	Off
12	10	FWT, Core	Ride 20 mi. (hilly)	SPD #7 Drills	BWT, Core Ride 20 mi. (fast)	10	Off
13	14	Cable, Core	Ride 25 mi.	SPD #8 Drills	MCH, Core Ride 20 mi. (fast)	8	Off
14	Ride 60 mi.	Combo, Core	TR 8	SPD #9 Drills	FWT, Core Ride 20 mi.(fast)	8	Off
15	20	Core	Ride 20 mi. (hilly)	SPD #10 Drills	Cable, Core Ride 20 mi. (fast)	8	Off
16	10	FWT, Core	Ride 30 mi.	SPD #11 Drills	MCH, Core Ride 20 mi. (fast)	8	Off
17	Ride 60 mi.	BWT, Core	TR 8	SPD #12 Drills	FWT, Core Ride 20 mi.	8	Off
18	20	Core	Ride 20 mi. (hilly)	SPD #13 Drills	MCH, Core Ride 20 mi. (fast)	8	Off
19	10	Combo, Core	Ride 20 mi.	SPD #14 Drills	Core Ride 30 mi.	8	Off
20	6	Ride 15 mi. Core	Off	SPD #15	Off	Drills	Off
21	MARATHON						

SPEED WORKOUTS

1-MILE WARM-UP, INTERVALS, 1-MILE COOLDOWN

1. 6 × 400 m
   with 200 m recoveries
   (5K race pace)

2. 400 m, 800 m, 400 m
   with 400 m recoveries
   (10K race pace)
   Repeat 3 times

3. 10 × 400 m
   with 200 m recoveries
   (5K race pace)

4. 400 m, 800 m, 1,200 m,
   800 m, 400 m
   with 400 m recoveries
   (10K race pace)
   Repeat 3 times

5. 6 × 800 m
   with 400 m recoveries
   (10K race pace)

6. 3 × 1,600 m
   with 400 m recoveries
   (10K race pace)

7. 8 × 800 m, 400 m
   with 400 m recoveries
   (10K race pace)

8. 3 × 1,600 m
   with 400 m recoveries
   (10K race pace)

9. 8 × 800 m
   with 400 m recoveries and a 5-
   minute rest after repeat number 5
   (10K race pace)

10. 4 × 1,600 m
    with 400 m recoveries
    (10K race pace)

11. 20 × 400 m
    with 200 m recoveries
    (5K race pace)

12. 400 m, 800 m, 1,200 m,
    800 m, 400 m
    with 400 m recoveries
    (10K race pace)
    Repeat 3 times

13. 4 × 1,600 m
    with 400 m recoveries
    (10K race pace)

14. 400 m, 800 m, 400 m, 800 m,
    400 m, 800 m, 400 m, 800 m,
    400 m
    with 400 m recoveries
    (10K race pace)
    Repeat 2 times

15. 4 × 200 m
    with 200 m recoveries
    (5K race pace)

KEY

LRR = Long Run or Ride   **STR** = Strength Training   **CORE** = Core Training   **X-TR** = Crosstraining
SPD = Speed Workout   **HW** = Hill Workout   **TR** = Tempo Run

MCH = Machine Workout   **FWT** = Free-Weight Workout   **BWT** = Body-Weight Workout
Combo = includes FWT, BWT, MCH, and Cable in the same workout

Note: *Run workouts are in bold. mi. = miles*

*At least one of your core workouts every week should include functional strength work, found in Ch. 4.

	TRAINING SCHEDULE						
+++	**COMPETITIVE MARATHON**						
WEEK	**SUN** LRR	**MON** STR/CORE*	**TUE** X-TR	**WED** SPD/HW	**THUR** STR/CORE/X-TR	**FRI** TR	**SAT** OFF
1	10	Cable, Core	Ride 25 mi. (hilly)	**HW x 4** Drills	MCH, Core Ride 25 mi. (fast)	7	Off
2	12	FWT, Core	Ride 25 mi. (hilly)	**HW x 6** Drills	BWT, Core Ride 25 mi. (fast)	7	Off
3	14	Cable, Core	Ride 25 mi. (hilly)	**HW x 6** Drills	MCH, Core Ride 25 mi. (fast)	8	Off
4	6	FWT, Core	Ride 25 mi. (hilly)	**HW x 8** Drills	BWT, Core Ride 25 mi. (fast)	8	Off
5	14	Cable, Core	Ride 25 mi. (hilly)	**HW x 8** Drills	MCH, Core Ride 25 mi. (fast)	8	Off
6	16	FWT, Core	Ride 30 mi. (hilly)	**SPD #1** Drills	BWT, Core Ride 30 mi. (fast)	8	Off
7	18	Cable, Core	Ride 30 mi. (hilly)	**SPD #2** Drills	MCH, Core Ride 30 mi. (fast)	8	Off
8	Ride 60 mi.	Combo, Core	**TR 10**	**SPD #3** Drills	FWT, Core Ride 30 mi. (fast)	8	Off
9	18	Cable, Core	Ride 30 mi. (hilly)	**SPD #4** Drills	MCH, Core Ride 30 mi. (fast)	8	Off
10	Ride 80 mi.	FWT, Core	**TR 8**	**SPD #5** Drills	BWT, Core Ride 30 mi. (fast)	8	Off
11	20	Cable, Core	Ride 30 mi. (hilly)	**SPD #6** Drills	MCH, Core Ride 30 mi. (fast)	8	Off
12	10	FWT, Core	Ride 30 mi. (hilly)	**SPD #7** Drills	BWT, Core Ride 30 mi. (fast)	10	Off
13	14	Cable, Core	Ride 30 mi. (hilly)	**SPD #8** Drills	MCH, Core Ride 30 mi. (fast)	8	Off
14	Ride 80 mi.	Combo, Core	**TR 8**	**SPD #9** Drills	FWT, Core Ride 30 mi. (fast)	8	Off
15	20	BWT, Core	Ride 30 mi. (hilly)	**SPD #10** Drills	Cable, Core Ride 30 mi. (fast)	8	Off
16	12	FWT, Core	Ride 30 mi.	**SPD #11** Drills	MCH, Core Ride 30 mi. (fast)	8	Off
17	Ride 80 mi.	BWT, Core	**TR 8**	**SPD #12** Drills	FWT, Core Ride 30 mi.	8	Off
18	22	Cable, Core	Ride 30 mi. (hilly)	**SPD #13** Drills	MCH, Core Ride 30 mi. (fast)	8	Off
19	10	Combo, Core	Ride 30 mi. (hilly)	**SPD #14** Drills	Core Ride 30 mi. (fast)	8	Off
20	6	Ride 25 mi. Core	Off	**SPD #15**	Off	Drills	Off
21	**MARATHON**						

SPEED WORKOUTS

1-MILE WARM-UP, INTERVALS, 1-MILE COOLDOWN

1. 8 × 400 m
   with 200 m recoveries
   (5K race pace)

2. 400 m, 800 m, 400 m
   with 400 m recoveries
   (10K race pace)
   Repeat 3 times

3. 10 × 400 m
   with 200 m recoveries
   (5K race pace)

4. 400 m, 800 m, 1,200 m,
   800 m, 400 m
   with 400 m recoveries
   (10K race pace)
   Repeat 3 times

5. 6 × 800 m
   with 400 m recoveries
   (10K race pace)

6. 4 × 1,600 m
   with 400 m recoveries
   (10K race pace)

7. 8 × 800 m, 400 m
   with 400 m recoveries
   (10K race pace)

8. 4 × 1,600 m
   with 400 m recoveries
   (10K race pace)

9. 10 × 800 m
   with 400 m recoveries and a 5-
   minute rest after repeat number 5
   (10K race pace)

10. 5 × 1,600 m
    with 400 m recoveries
    (10K race pace)

11. 20 × 400 m
    with 200 m recoveries
    (5K race pace)

12. 400 m, 800 m, 1,200 m,
    800 m, 400 m
    with 400 m recoveries
    (10K race pace)
    Repeat 3 times

13. 6 × 1,600 m
    with 400 m recoveries
    (10K race pace)

14. 400 m, 800 m, 400 m, 800 m,
    400 m, 800 m, 400 m, 800 m,
    400 m
    with 400 m recoveries
    (10K race pace)
    Repeat 2 times

15. 4 × 400 m
    with 200 m recoveries
    (5K race pace)

KEY

LRR = Long Run or Ride   STR = Strength Training   CORE = Core Training   X-TR = Crosstraining
SPD = Speed Workout   HW = Hill Workout   TR = Tempo Run

MCH = Machine Workout   FWT = Free-Weight Workout   BWT = Body-Weight Workout
Combo = includes FWT, BWT, MCH, and Cable in the same workout

Note: *Run workouts are in bold. mi. = miles*

*At least one of your core workouts every week should include functional strength work, found in Ch. 4.

Epilogue
THINKING LIKE A COACH

MY WIFE, STEPHANIE, IS A FOODIE. She loves the taste, aroma, and texture of food and the challenge of taking a bunch of raw ingredients and transforming them into something mouthwatering. When she takes up the challenge of preparing a new dish, she lays out the recipe on the kitchen counter, faithfully tracking the recipe's instructions, trusting that by the time she completes the journey, she will have successfully achieved her goal.

That isn't the way my grandmother cooked. She'd add a pinch of this and a handful of that, using intuition and experience to tell her when she had gotten it right.

By this point, if you've faithfully read this book and implemented the workouts it contains, you've stocked up your running kitchen with everything you need to prepare a perfect race. But if you're like most runners, there's likely two things that are missing here that my grandmother had while cooking: faith in your own knowledge and effort, along with confidence in your own intuition, borne of experience, to know when you've gotten it all just right.

You could, of course, follow every detail in one of the training programs here and get to the starting line confident that you did everything just right in preparing for your target race. That's perfectly fine. In all likelihood, that would result in one of your best race-day efforts.

But we're aiming here for more than that. Think of this book not as a series of set workouts and routines but instead as a guide to thinking like a coach. Just as you can look at a cookbook as a compendium of suggestions and ideas, you should look at this book as providing the range of tools and workouts for you to dip into as needed.

Don't focus on the number of repetitions or intervals at the expense of understanding how the entire plan fits together. Numbers are surely important, but not as important as absorbing the way in which the workouts add up to make you a stronger, better athlete.

Here's an example of what I mean: Sometimes a tight schedule forces me to deviate a bit from my workout plan. A long bike ride might end up being 5 miles short of my workout goal. The regimented part of my brain screams in protest, knowing that too many shortcuts can lead to insufficient preparation and race-day disappointment. But the rational side of my brain knows that if I pushed hard in the miles that I did ride, then the workout hit my goal of maintaining my endurance base and varying the kind of workouts that I do. The workout may not have been perfect, but it was good enough.

Sometimes good enough is good enough.

To look at this a different way, consider the approach taken by many elite athletes. The best runners know their bodies well enough to be able to gauge the fitness of their bodies without strictly adhering to a training plan. They never let a training plan trump the reality of what they feel. If they need a day off, they take it, confident that in the long run they will be all the stronger for the change from their set routine.

This reminds me of an article I once read about the way in which some drivers had become slaves to their GPS systems. A large number of drivers had gotten themselves into trouble by following GPS directions instead of relying on what they were seeing on the road. Some drove into the woods; others went into a snowbank or stream. When asked why they had done so, they replied, "That's what [the GPS] told me to do."

I was dumbfounded when I read that. Personally, I don't care if it's the voice of God Almighty telling me to make a left; if I see the road is washed out, I'm hitting the brakes and turning around.

Don't let this training guide—or any training guide—lead you off a cliff. Be your own best coach by following these simple guidelines:

- Understand the workouts and why you are supposed to do them.
- Make sure that you cover the bases in your training by implementing all of the elements of the program somewhere, in a sensible, purposeful fashion.
- Don't worry about nailing every workout down to the second. That's not what proper race preparation is really about.
- Work hard, but don't confuse fatigue and soreness with fitness.
- Don't ignore your body's signals; trust your body when it tells you that it's had a good workout, regardless of the numbers you posted. With the right effort and recovery, the numbers will all work out in the end.

Before you close the book and head out the door for your run, I want you to think about one more thing: Consider why you run.

Not long ago I found myself at a conference on running and running injuries. Around me in the conference room were leading researchers from across the globe, brilliant scientists who were sharing the very latest studies and findings on what happens to our bodies when we run.

At one point during the weekend, we attended an open meeting with the general public where we were to lead a discussion about running. I had wondered whether anyone would attend, but I need not have worried: We arrived to a large room filled to capacity, with people spilling over into the adjoining hallway.

Twelve of us were invited to sit at the dais and give brief presentations to the crowd. We were not given any guidelines or restrictions; each of us could just say whatever came to mind.

As luck had it, I sat near the end of the line. The presenters before me all talked about theories on injury and proper form. All the comments were insightful and helpful; these were people who knew their stuff. But when it was finally my turn to speak, I realized that, although all of the presenters had spoken about *how* to run, no one had talked about *why* we run.

This was, I thought, a problem. Even though running surely promotes cardiovascular fitness, core strength, weight control, mood elevation, and a host of other positive side effects, marathon running is a completely different animal. Marathoners are no doubt fit, but no one needs to run a marathon in order to get fit. That goal can be attained on far less mileage.

Marathon training and racing can actually be potentially dangerous activities. It almost goes without saying, then, that marathoners run for very different reasons than recreational runners do. Nevertheless, as marathoners, we rarely seem to take the time to really ask ourselves exactly why it is we run as much as we do.

In my remarks at the public meeting, I urged all the people in the room to ask themselves why they run. It wasn't a frivolous question, I told them, because late in the marathon, when our bodies are tired and sore and begging to stop, when no one would blame us for stopping, the science of running and the details of our training schedules won't be what helps motivate us to keep moving forward. At that moment, we'll need to dig deeper to find a reason to push on. Whether it's the memory of a loved one or a need to prove that we can persist when others would give up, each of us needs to tap into that intangible something, that force that enables us to step outside the ordinary into the heroic.

With this book, I have aimed to give you the tools you need to become the kind of runner you want to be. But they are only tools. To make the most of your running, you will need to take them and make them your own, to use them alongside the gifts that you—all of us—possess as runners and individuals and the motivation that you possess to keep going forward when others would stop.

Good luck and keep running!

Appendix A:
RACE PACE CHART

TO SET REALISTIC AND ACHIEVABLE RACE GOALS, you need to know the average pace at which you've run your best and most recent races, as well as the average pace you must run in order to attain your goal race time. This chart indicates the paces associated with various finishing times. Use it to figure out what you've already accomplished, as well as to see what it will take for you to hit your target finishing time. Locate your best race times—as closely as possible—within the available race distances listed in the vertical columns. This is your base speed. Remember that your pace for a 5K, for example, should naturally be faster than your pace for longer distances, such as a marathon. Pace should fluctuate with distance. If you don't see much variation in your pace across different distances, use this information to determine whether you need to work more on endurance to sustain the speed you showed in short races, or more on speed to take advantage of the endurance you showed in the longer races.

It is important to note that these are average minutes-per-mile paces. Not even the best elite runners churn out mile after mile at the exact same pace (although many come close). Your mile split times will vary depending on elevation changes on the course, altitude, and weather, as well as your own surging and ebbing energy levels.

RACE PACE CHART

PACE PER MILE	3.1 MILES (5K)	5 MILES	6.2 MILES (10K)	10 MILES	HALF-MARATHON	MARATHON
5:30	17:05	27:30	34:11	55:00	1:12:06	2:24:12
5:45	17:52	28:45	35:44	57:30	1:15:23	2:30:46
6:00	18:39	30:00	37:17	1:00:00	1:18:39	2:37:19
6:15	19:25	31:15	38:50	1:02:30	1:21:56	2:43:52
6:30	20:12	32:30	40:23	1:05:00	1:25:13	2:50:25
6:45	20:58	33:45	41:57	1:07:30	1:28:29	2:56:59
7:00	21:45	35:00	43:30	1:10:00	1:31:46	3:03:32
7:15	22:32	36:15	45:03	1:12:30	1:35:02	3:10:05
7:30	23:18	37:30	46:36	1:15:00	1:38:19	3:16:39
7:45	24:05	38:45	48:10	1:17:30	1:41:36	3:23:12
8:00	24:51	40:00	49:43	1:20:00	1:44:52	3:29:45
8:15	25:38	41:15	51:16	1:22:30	1:48:09	3:36:18
8:30	26:25	42:30	52:49	1:25:00	1:51:26	3:42:52
8:45	27:11	43:45	54:22	1:27:30	1:54:42	3:49:25
9:00	27:58	45:00	55:56	1:30:00	1:57:59	3:55:58
9:15	28:44	46:15	57:29	1:32:30	2:01:15	4:02:32
9:30	29:31	47:30	59:02	1:35:00	2:04:32	4:09:05
9:45	30:18	48:45	1:00:35	1:37:30	2:07:49	4:15:38
10:00	31:04	50:00	1:02:08	1:40:00	2:11:05	4:22:11
10:30	32:37	52:30	1:05:15	1:45:00	2:17:39	4:35:18
11:00	34:11	55:00	1:08:21	1:50:00	2:24:12	4:48:25
11:30	35:44	57:30	1:11:28	1:55:00	2:30:45	5:01:31

Appendix B:
RATE OF PERCEIVED EXERTION

TO GET THE MOST FROM YOUR TRAINING, you must be able to gauge your effort level. If you knew your resting heart rate and your true maximum heart rate, you could track your effort by monitoring your beats per minute during workouts. A cheaper and often equally effective method is to check in periodically with how you feel while training and racing. Most people can identify various gradations in their effort levels with great accuracy. The trick is to know which effort level you should be in for each workout and to stay within that zone. Use the chart below to help you.

RATE OF PERCEIVED EXERTION			
LEVEL	LEVEL OF EFFORT AND EFFECTS	SUSTAINABLE PERIOD	APPLICABLE WORKOUT
1–4	No effort to very mild effort	Indefinite	Sleeping, grocery shopping
5–7	Easy effort; breaking a sweat, breathing a little heavier	With proper training and nutritional support, up to 24 hours or more	Easy pace for the long run
8	Harder effort; heavier breathing and sweating	Up to target race distance/3–4 hours	Tempo run, easy hills
9	Heavy breathing; fairly rapid onset of fatigue	Shorter periods generally up to 1 hour	Hills, speed work
10	Very heavy breathing; rapid onset of burning in muscles, rapid loss of power and form	Approximately 1–2 minutes	Short sprints, escape from a burning building

References

Burgomaster, K. A., S. C. Hughes, G. J. Heigenhauser, S. N. Bradwell, and M. J. Gibala. 2005. "Six Sessions of Sprint Interval Training Increases Muscle Oxidative Potential and Cycle Endurance Capacity in Humans." *Journal of Applied Physiology* 98 (6): 1985–90. http://www.ncbi.nlm.nih.gov/pubmed/15705728.

Daniels, Jack. n.d. "Running Training: Principles and Needs." http://www.coacheseducation.com/endur/jack-daniels-june-00.htm.

———. 2005. *Daniels' Running Formula*, 2nd ed. Champaign, IL: Human Kinetics.

Eyestone, Ed. 2007. "How Many Miles a Week Should I Run?" *Runner's World*, July 24.

Fowles, J. R., D. G. Sale, and J. D. MacDougall. 200. "Reduced Strength after Passive Stretch of the Human Plantarflexors." *Journal of Applied Physiology* 89 (2000): 1179–88.

Gibala, M. J., J. P. Little, M. van Essen, G. P. Wilkin, K. A. Burgomaster, A. Safdar, S. Raha, and M. A. Tarnopolsky. 2006. "Short-Term Sprint Interval Versus Traditional Endurance Training: Similar Initial Adaptations in Human Skeletal Muscle and Exercise Performance." *Journal of Physiology* 575: 901–11. www.ncbi.nlm.nih.gov/pubmed/16825308.

Graham, T. E., L. P. Turcotte, B. Kiens, and E. A. Richter. 1995. "Training and Muscle Ammonia and Amino Acid Metabolism in Humans During Prolonged Exercise." *Journal of Applied Physiology* 78 (2): 725–35.

Haskell, W. L., I. Lee, R. R. Pate et al. 2007. "Physical Activity and Public Health: Updated Recommendation for Adults from the American College of Sports Medicine and the American Heart Association." *Circulation: Journal of the American Heart Association.* 116: 1081–93.

Jackson, E. Newton, Brian M. Hickey, and Virden Evans. 2009. "Using the Tabata Protocol to Improve Aerobic Capacity." Florida A&M University, Tallahassee, Florida. http://aahperd.confex.com/aahperd/2009/finalprogram/paper_12959.htm.

Noakes, Tim, MD. 2003. *The Lore of Running*, 4th ed. Cape Town, South Africa: Oxford University Press.

Pfitzinger, Pete, MS. 2006. "Improving Your Stride Rate." *Running Times Magazine*, September.

van Gent, R. N., D. Siem, M. van Middelkoop, A. G. van Os, S. M. A. Bierma-Zeinstra, B. W. Koes. 2007. "Incidence and Determinants of Lower Extremity Running Injuries in Long Distance Runners: A Systematic Review." *British Journal of Sports Medicine* 41: 469–80. http://bjsm.bmj.com/content/41/8/469.full.pdf.

Index

Note: f. indicates figure; t. indicates table.

About the Author

 **JEFF HOROWITZ** ran his first marathon in 1987 and fell in love with the sport. Since then, he's run over 150 marathons and ultramarathons, doing at least one in every state in the U.S. and also around the world, from Antarctica to Africa to Asia. Formerly a practicing attorney, he now works as a program director for Achieve Kids Tri, Inc., a D.C.-based nonprofit that introduces at-risk kids throughout the country to a healthy lifestyle through the sport of triathlon. Jeff is also a certifed personal trainer and running, cycling, and triathlon coach (AFAA, USAT, US-ATF, USA Cycling, and RRCA certified). He has been the Mid-Atlantic editor of *Competitor* magazine, and a frequent contributer to *Marathon & Beyond* as well as other publications. His book, *My First 100 Marathons: 2,620 Miles with an Obsessive Runner* was released in 2008. Jeff is married to the artist Stephanie Kay, with whom he has a 6-year-old son, Alex Michael.